Prayer:
Your own letter to God

Prayer:
Your own letter to God

ANDRÉ K. DUGGER

ZONDERVAN.com/
AUTHORTRACKER
follow your favorite authors

ZONDERVAN

Prayer: Your Own Letter to God
Copyright © 2010 by André K. Dugger

This title is also available as a Zondervan ebook.
Visit www.zondervan.com/ebooks.

This title is also available in a Zondervan audio edition.
Visit www.zondervan.fm.

Requests for information should be addressed to:
Zondervan, *Grand Rapids, Michigan 49530*

Library of Congress Cataloging-in-Publication Data

Dugger, André K., 1963-
    Prayer: your own letter to God : a practical prayer guide inspired by the major
    motion picture, Letters to God / André K. Dugger.
        p. cm.
    Includes bibliographical references.
    ISBN 978-0-310-32763-9 (softcover)
    1. Prayer — Christianity. 2. Letter writing — Religious aspects — Christianity. I. Title.
BV215.D83 2010
    248.3'2 — dc22   2009051059

Published in association with the literary agency of Wolgemuth & Associates, Inc.

Interior design: Michelle Espinoza

Printed in the United States of America

10 11 12 13 14 15 16 • 23 22 21 20 19 18 17 16 15 14 13 12 11 10 9 8 7 6 5 4 3 2 1

The movie Letters to God *was inspired by a wonderful little boy, Tyler Doughtie, whom I had the privilege of knowing and loving. Before he went to be with the Lord, Tyler wrote letters to God as one way of praying during his battle with cancer. My prayer is that his legacy will inspire you as much as it has me. This book is dedicated to his memory.*

I also dedicate this book to my wife, Sarah, and our children, Jed, Josh, Caylee, Joseph, James, and Caitlyn.

Finally, I dedicate this book to my two sets of parents, Wilburn and Jo Yvonne Dugger and Jack and Lou Barron, who by their own prayer lives helped teach me how to pray. After my birth parents died, Jack and Lou put feet to their prayers as they willingly brought me and my two brothers into their family, which already included three boys. Thank you, Mom and Dad, for living out your prayers through faithful lives.

Contents

Acknowledgments

A project like this book is possible only when a team of people work together to make it a reality. I give all the glory to God for every positive result from this book. My new friends at Zondervan, David Frees and Brian Phipps, have been a blessing to work with. My literary agent, Robert Wolgemuth, and his entire team worked diligently to ensure this book and all of our *Letters to God* products came to fruition. Michael Ranville, who ran point on this project, made it all come together.

Lyn Cryderman came alongside me at the eleventh hour and helped make this book complete. I am indebted to Lyn for all he did.

My dear friends Patrick and Heather Doughtie were extremely generous in allowing me to share in the entire *Letters to God* project. I owe them a huge amount of gratitude, and I look forward to working with them on many future projects.

A big thank-you goes to our church family, Grace Baptist of Nashville, Tennessee, for their love and support. I have been blessed through the years with many wonderful churches, pastors, and friends in the ministry who have helped make me who I am and who have helped shape my prayer life. God has blessed me with wonderful associates, administrative assistants, and pastor colleagues who have encouraged me to faithfully fulfill God's call on my life.

Author Dan Miller has become a wonderful friend. Our relationship began with my reading his books *48 Days to the Work You Love* and *No More Mondays* and grew as he became a personal coach for Sarah and me. Dan, thank you for your support and encouragement to go out and fulfill the calling God has placed on my life.

Writing a book takes a lot of time. The process is much easier when you are blessed with quiet places to write. Through the years, several families have graciously provided either financial assistance or the use of their homes and cabins to allow me the opportunity to do what God has called me to do. Being in a beautiful setting sure makes it easier to write.

Two special ladies deserve a word of appreciation. Jill Thompson has been an incredible help with her transcription work, and Carolyn Gregory has always been willing to assist me with editing. Thank you for all you do.

I mentioned my two sets of parents in the dedication; I also want to mention the rest of my family. I have been blessed with five super brothers — Ronnie, Ricky, Richard, Randy, and Verrall — and their families, as well as wonderful in-laws, aunts, uncles, cousins, and grandparents. They have prayed for my family and me through the years, and I do not take for granted any one of these wonderful people and the manner in which God has used them in my life. Thank you to each and every one of you.

The one person who deserves the most credit and appreciation is my incredible wife, Sarah. Sarah is more than just my wife; she is my best friend, my lover, the mother of our six children, my partner in everything I do, and the biggest encourager I have ever had. This book would not exist without her. Sarah is an incredible writer, and God is using her to bless others more than she will ever realize. I love you, Sarah, and I appreciate you and our children (Jed, Joshua, Caylee, Joseph, James, and Caitlyn) for helping me with this book and being patient during this process.

Understanding Prayer

A little boy dying of cancer asks God to help his new mailman, who is a cynical alcoholic. The little boy's family and friends ask God to heal him of his disease. The mailman discovers God's love for him and cleans up his life, while the little boy loses his battle with cancer. Few things in our lives are at once so simple yet complex as the subject of prayer. What is prayer? How does it work? *Does* it work? Whose prayers get answered and why? What do we know for sure about prayer?

I don't have all the answers, but the Bible clearly teaches us that God wants His children to pray to Him and that He always answers our prayers. In part 1 of this book, we will closely examine prayer to determine what it really is and how you can make it a dynamic part of your walk with God.

Why We Pray

I cannot prove this, but I believe that all people have attempted to pray at least once in their lives. People who grew up in church probably had a parent who said a bedtime prayer with them at night, such as "Now I lay me down to sleep." You might have learned how to pray by listening to your parents pray, by saying grace before a family dinner, by going to Sunday school or some other form of religious education, or by spending a lot of Sundays in church. Among Christians who attend church regularly, prayer is familiar. Even in a culture as diverse as ours, it would be hard to find someone who has never prayed in some fashion or who does not know what prayer is to some degree.

Even if you've never set foot inside a church building or other religious facility, you know something about prayer. Back when prayer in school became a divisive argument, someone jokingly observed that as long as teachers give pop quizzes, there will always be prayer in school. There is some truth to that. When faced with an overwhelming challenge or burden, even people who otherwise have no interest in religion often bow their heads or ask a friend to pray for them. This instinctive turning to prayer gives way to the phrase "There are no atheists in foxholes."

Even the most irreligious people are inclined at least to attempt to pray in times of deep personal turmoil or tragedy. Tragic events such as the terrorist attacks on the World Trade Center on September 11, 2001, and Hurricane Katrina sent many otherwise secular citizens to their knees. And while no one would mistake most network news reporters for prayer warriors, when reporting from the scene of a disaster, they often end their reports with something like, "Our prayers are with their families."

It seems that virtually everyone is driven to pray at some point.

Someone's Listening

Most of the time, our prayers are specifically for something or someone. We pray for a job after we have been laid off. We pray for a loan to be approved. We pray for the test results from the lab to show that we are healthy. We pray for our children when they head off to school. We pray for our aging parents. We pray for a friend going through a difficult time. That we pray for these types of things suggests one of the major reasons people pray: we believe someone is listening. Of course, Christians pray with the assurance that God is listening. Throughout the Old Testament, we see God's children—the Israelites—calling out to God in prayer. In a poignant message delivered by the prophet Jeremiah, God reassured His followers that "you will call upon me and come and pray to me, and I will listen to you" (Jer. 29:12). The psalmist wrote, "The LORD accepts my prayer" (Ps. 6:9).

It's comforting to know that the Creator of the universe cares about us and is somehow able to hear our prayer along with millions of others. Although some of the comedy goes too far for my tastes, the movie *Bruce Almighty* has a funny scene in which actor Jim Carrey finds himself in a room in heaven where all the prayers of mankind arrive, and he is comically overwhelmed with the flood of people's prayers from "down below." It's impossible for the human mind to fully grasp how prayer works, but that doesn't stop us from praying. Do you remember when you were a child and you wanted to talk to your daddy? You didn't stop to wonder if he was listening or not, or if he really wanted to answer your endless questions. You just asked away, trusting that he was paying attention to you and had yet another answer. That's what it's like between us and God. When we need something that seems beyond our reach, we pray out of a simple faith that God is listening.

Praying Like Jesus

Another reason Christians pray is that we want to become more and more like Jesus. As Christians, we are really "Christ ones," people who not only identify with Jesus but strive to become like Him. As we observe the life of Jesus as recorded in the New Testament, we cannot help but notice the significance He placed on prayer. Jesus practiced a powerful prayer life, and He wants us to do the same. Christians pray because Jesus did; it was an important resource for His ministry. In fact, He even taught us how to pray in what has perhaps become the most frequently recited prayer of all time: the Lord's Prayer. Throughout His life on earth, Jesus prayed often. Prayer is important to us because it was important to Jesus.

Prior to Jesus' coming to the earth, He and His Father had enjoyed each other's company for all eternity. But then, to fulfill God's master plan for mankind, Jesus left the glory of heaven to become a man on earth. Jesus was fully God the Son, the second member of the Trinity, and He was fully man at the same time. Because of His humanity, He experienced emotions of loneliness and a yearning to be with His Father. Until that point, Jesus and His Father had always been together. When Jesus left the splendor of heaven, He still strove to maintain their relationship even though He was no longer physically present with His Father. He did that through prayer, modeling for us how we can have a relationship with God even though we are not physically in His presence. Philip Yancey, author of *Prayer: Does It Make Any Difference?* describes prayer as being more "companionship" than "transaction," and this is evident in Jesus' example. He prayed to stay in touch, not just to ask for things, and many Christians describe praying as "spending time with the Lord." We pray because it allows us to sense God's presence more fully. As the humble eighteenth-century monk Brother Lawrence wrote, "There is not in the world a kind of life more sweet and delightful than that of a continual conversation with God."

A related reason we pray is that it draws us closer to God. At its very core, prayer is fellowship and communication with God. It is a wonderful way to "be with God," much like Jesus' staying connected to God during His ministry on earth. He was separated physically from His Father, but He stayed close to Him through prayer. Christians have the blessed hope of spending eternity in the physical presence of God, but through prayer, we also can enjoy His presence as we go about our daily business on earth. I can be with God even when I am in my car on the way to an appointment. I can start every day sitting in my favorite chair, watching the sunrise, and enjoy a special time simply basking in His presence. An old hymn says, "And he walks with me and talks with me," and that's a perfect explanation of why prayer is so vital to our spiritual growth. Prayer maintains the intimate, personal relationship between the believer and the Almighty, a once unfathomable distance between heaven and earth now bridged by the outstretched arms of Jesus on the cross.

We also learn from Jesus that prayer served as the foundation of His ministry. His first recorded act following His transition into His public ministry was to spend time in prayer with His Father. One day when John the Baptist was preaching about the coming Messiah and baptizing those who believed, Jesus came to him to be baptized. Consider the following passage from the book of Luke: "When all the people were being baptized, Jesus was baptized too. And as he was praying, heaven was opened and the Holy Spirit descended on him in bodily form like a dove. And a voice came from heaven: 'You are my Son, whom I love; with you I am well pleased' " (Luke 3:21–23).

This shows us Jesus' desire to talk with His Father before He embarked on His earthly ministry. If prayer was that important to Jesus, shouldn't it be just as crucial for us?

People sometimes make fun of athletes who make the sign of the cross before stepping into the batter's box or who kneel in the end zone after scoring a touchdown, but why shouldn't prayer be the first thing we think of both when we face something difficult and when we celebrate something good? I will leave it up to God to determine if these public expressions are sincere, but we all would benefit from making prayer a natural, regular, and frequent activity in our lives. Jesus' act of praying at the beginning of His ministry demonstrates the emphasis He placed on prayer, both for Himself and, by example, for His followers.

You've probably seen the commercial in which something dramatic interrupts, say, a husband and wife relaxing in their living room, and the tagline is, "Life comes at you fast." Even though I can't recall the product being advertised, I can really relate to that tagline, which raises the question, Shouldn't we be more like the baseball and football players and spend more time praying? Though the quick symbolic prayer is not what we're after, do we really want to go it alone when God has invited us to bring *all* of our cares to Him?

I know an old story that illustrates this point. Once there was an older factory worker who prayed to God for just about everything. Many people thought he was a little eccentric. As he got in his car to drive to work, he would say out loud, "Lord, let this car start today." When he punched in at work, his fellow employees laughed as he again prayed out loud, "Lord, help me do Your work today." If something good happened to him—say, his boss let him leave early—he immediately breathed a quick, "Thank you, Lord." One day his son-in-law was driving him somewhere, and the car just quit. Instinctively, the old man matter-of-factly prayed, "Lord, please teach my daughter's husband to always check the gas gauge before he takes me anywhere." When his son-in-law asked him why he didn't pray for someone to come along with a can of gas, the old man smiled and said, "I save those prayers for me."

As Augustine reportedly once wrote, "Pray as though everything depends on God. Work as though everything depends on you."

Strength for Today

In addition to praying at the outset of His ministry, Jesus demonstrated the significance of regular prayer. He often went out into the countryside to

spend time alone with His Father in prayer. This models for us the importance of developing a consistent prayer life rather than turning to God in
prayer only when we're in trouble or have a pressing need. Parents of college students who live away from home joke that the only time they hear
from their kids is when they need money. But that's what a lot of us do with
God. We're "away from home" during our brief time on earth, and as long as
everything is going well, we spend very little time in prayer. But the minute
we need something, we're on our knees, begging God for help. Jesus knew
that to fulfill His ministry, He needed regular times of conversation with His
Father. We too have a ministry on earth: to proclaim the good news of salvation; to feed and clothe the hungry; to love the unlovely; and, in the name
of Christ, to help "the least of these." Prolific nineteenth-century Christian
writer Andrew Murray described prayer as "a force that can move the heavenly world, and can bring its power down to earth." Just as Jesus used regular
times of prayer to sustain Him for His ministry, we need to tap into that same
resource if we want to fulfill our calling as Christians. In fact, in reflecting
on my own ministry and the great spiritual awakenings in history, I cannot
think of any significant movement of God in the lives of people that was not
preceded by regular, fervent prayer. As evangelist Dwight L. Moody once said,
"Every great movement of God can be traced to a kneeling figure."

I find it interesting and instructive that the main thing we know about
Jesus and prayer is that He often did it alone. In fact, in His Sermon on the
Mount, He warns against praying elaborate prayers in public to show off our
religiosity. As a pastor, I consider it a privilege to lead my congregation in
prayer on Sunday mornings. Until recently, many churches had midweek
"prayer meetings," when the faithful would gather for one purpose: to pray as
a group for the needs of their community and the world. Clearly, corporate
prayer has a place, but Jesus often demonstrated the importance of private
prayer. The Bible tells us that after Jesus performed the miracle of feeding
more than five thousand people, and "after he had dismissed them, he went
up on a mountainside by himself to pray. When evening came, he was there
alone" (Matt. 14:23). Immediately following this incredible miracle of turning
a little boy's small lunch into a massive meal that fed a multitude, Jesus went
off alone to spend time with His Father in prayer. In Mark's gospel, we see
Jesus setting aside another special time to be alone in prayer: "Very early in
the morning, while it was still dark, Jesus got up, left the house and went off
to a solitary place, where he prayed" (Mark 1:35).

Why did Jesus go off by Himself to pray after performing a miracle? We
can only guess, but from my experience as a pastor, I know that caring for

others' needs often depletes my spiritual resources. People in the helping professions often suffer burnout, and every Christian is in the helping profession. Jesus' example teaches us that prayer is essential to ministry. We cannot pour ourselves into others without stopping regularly to replenish our spirits by spending time alone with God.

A friend of mine told me the story of a journalist who earlier in his career covered several Billy Graham crusades. As he became familiar with Dr. Graham and his team, he was granted greater access to the behind-the-scenes aspects of these incredible events. Once, in Hong Kong, he positioned himself behind the platform, hoping to speak with the evangelist as he left the stadium. After the choir finished the last verse of that trademark invitation hymn "Just As I Am" and those who came forward were assigned to spiritual counselors who could explain the plan of salvation, Dr. Graham emerged through a small opening and immediately stopped to pray. "I couldn't bring myself to interrupt him because it just seemed as if he was soaking up all the strength and energy he had given when he preached to the thousands who had come to hear him," the journalist recounted.

I can't imagine not praying. When you stop and think about it, prayer is one of the great privileges of the Christian life. Just as salvation is a gift freely offered, prayer is similarly given to us so that we don't have to face the trials of life on our own. Yet most Christians struggle with their prayer life. They know that praying is something they should do, but most feel they don't do it enough. When being interviewed about the writing of his book *Prayer*, Philip Yancey spoke about the contrast between the great number of bestselling books about prayer and the great number of the people who expressed to him their frustration over prayer.

While I believe everyone — or nearly everyone — attempts to pray, I also know that far too many people don't pray as much as they would like to. If God uses prayer to mold us into being more like Jesus, sustain us to fulfill our calling as Christians, comfort us when we are sad, and bring us into His very presence, why *don't* we pray more?

Why We Stop Praying

One of the most common concerns I hear from my church members and friends is their frustration about praying, or more accurately, their struggle to pray. Most Christians know that they should pray regularly, but few that I know of report success at developing a consistent, meaningful prayer life. When things aren't going well, we tend to pray often and earnestly. When things get back to normal, either we spend very little time in prayer or the praying that we do is almost rote, certainly not as intimate and focused as when we are facing difficult times and need help. My prayer is that God will use this book to help make you the exception to the rule.

Perhaps this story from Jill will sound familiar to you. Jill, in her early forties, is a wife and mother who recently reentered the workforce as a classroom teacher's aid. She stayed at home with her two boys until the youngest entered middle school. Her husband is a sales rep for a steel supply company, and about twice a month, he has to be out of town for a couple of days. Her family is active in church; they're one of those families you can always count on to volunteer and to support the church financially. Jill is on the youth group's parent council, and she and her husband serve as greeters every Sunday morning in church. You couldn't find a more loyal and devoted Christian family. Yet Jill struggles with prayer.

"I believe in prayer," Jill carefully explained. "And I know I ought to pray more, but sometimes it just seems like I'm mumbling words without thinking or that I'm just going through the motions. Sometimes I get discouraged because I pray for something and nothing happens. I don't really get angry at God or anything because I've been taught that what I want isn't always what God wants for me. But after a while I just seem to quit praying. Praying for me is sort of like riding a roller coaster; sometimes I get in the habit of praying every day, then I stop praying for a while, then it's back to praying again."

As I said, Jill is one of the pillars of her church. She's not a new Christian who is trying to learn about prayer but a woman who has spent her adult life as an active church member. She knows all about prayer, has heard dozens of sermons on the topic, participates in her church's prayer chain, and even prays with her family before meals and during family devotions. Yet her personal experience with prayer is hit-and-miss.

Jill's story reminds me of a man who seems to have had a similar experience with prayer. One day he would excitedly report how God had answered his prayers miraculously, then the next day he would be all down in the dumps because he felt God had completely forsaken him. His name was David, the king of ancient Israel and the person whom God used to author much of the Old Testament book of Psalms. Consider just a sampling of his thoughts on prayer.

O LORD, heal me, for my bones are in agony. My soul is in anguish. How long, O LORD, how long?... I am worn out from groaning; all night long I flood my bed with weeping and drench my couch with tears.

—Psalm 6:2–3, 6

Why, O LORD, do you stand far off? Why do you hide yourself in times of trouble?

—Psalm 10:1

How long, O LORD? Will you forget me forever?

—Psalm 13:1

My God, my God, why have you forsaken me? Why are you so far from saving me, so far from the words of my groaning? O my God, I cry out by day, but you do not answer.

—Psalm 22:1–2

Sounds like a guy who has given up on prayer, right? But read on.

In my distress I called to the LORD; I cried to my God for help. From his temple he heard my voice; my cry came before him, into his ears.... He reached down from on high and took hold of me; he drew me out of deep waters.

—Psalm 18:6, 16

O LORD my God, I called to you for help and you healed me.

—Psalm 30:2

I sought the LORD, and he answered me; he delivered me from all my fears.

—Psalm 34:4

But I call to God, and the LORD saves me. Evening, morning and noon I cry out in distress, and he hears my voice.... Cast your cares on the LORD and he will sustain you; he will never let the righteous fall.

—Psalm 55:16–17, 22

Prayer As a Supernatural Activity

What do David, Jill, you, and I all have in common? Prayer often frustrates us. When it works the way we want it to, we love it and want to tell everyone about the way God came through for us. When it doesn't, we get discouraged, even a little upset or impatient. Many of us, like Jill and David, let that discouragement lead us into a drought; if we pray at all, it is merely lip service.

Part of the reason so many of us approach prayer with a certain degree of ambivalence is that it takes us out of our everyday world and moves us into the realm of the supernatural. Since the Enlightenment, and especially since the gigantic strides made in scientific discovery and technology beginning in the twentieth century, rationalism has influenced thinking about prayer and about all things spiritual. For many people, praying and expecting results is a little primitive, almost superstitious, like carrying around a rabbit's foot and believing it brings you good luck. One minute you're shaving and getting ready for work; the next minute you're sitting by yourself, talking to someone who is not visibly present and who some people say doesn't exist. To the rational mind, it doesn't compute, and sometimes that way of thinking creeps into our own thoughts about prayer. Certainly, as a Christian, you trust the encouraging instruction to "fix our eyes not on what is seen, but on what is unseen" (2 Cor. 4:18). Intuitively, you understand the whole concept about God being present through His Spirit and that He loves to hear from His children. And you know that His Word instructs you to ask for whatever you want in accordance with His will, and He will give it to you. But intellectually, your mind pulls you back into the rational world. Can He really hear me? How can He distinguish between my voice and the millions of others calling out to Him at this very moment? If He really promised to give you what you ask for, why wasn't your son healed of his leukemia when you prayed so hard for him?

I have asked similar questions at various times in my life, and here's what I find interesting. Whenever we pray to God and He answers the way we want Him to answer, we have no difficulty accepting the supernatural, nor do we try to second-guess God. We do not attribute His answer to our prayer as coincidence but truly believe that He heard our prayer and answered it. Just because we don't get exactly what we ask for doesn't mean that God isn't listening or that prayer doesn't "work." Prayer isn't a good-luck charm that guarantees we will get what we want; if it were, all of us would be millionaires by now. God is sovereign and knows what is best for us, and if we are faithful, He will always give us exactly what we need, which may not be what we want Him to give us. Prayer is more about a relationship with God than about a laundry list of things we want Him to do. Whenever I become discouraged because God seems to be ignoring one of my prayers, I remind myself that my relationship with God is what's important and continue praying. I have felt the closest to God during those times and have realized that in addition to giving me the privilege of being in His presence, He is teaching me patience and trust. Through this "wrestling with God," I emerge with a sense of peace and reassurance that He loves me, that He knows what He is doing, and that the outcome, whatever it might be, will be perfect.

As a young child, I prayed every night before I went to bed, asking God to protect my mother and father and not to let them die. I am not sure why I was so focused on the fact that they might die, but I was. On July 4, 1976, three months before I turned thirteen, I returned from a fireworks show to discover that my mother had died. I was devastated and angry at God. I can remember going outside and screaming at Him, "God, why would You let my mama die?" I said, "God, there are thousands of prostitutes who could die today and nobody would miss them or care. Why would You let my mama die?"

Less than four years later, my father went to be with the Lord. I was sixteen, and both of my parents had left me and gone to heaven. All those years of praying for God to protect my mother and father, and the last four years of praying for my father alone, seemed wasted. I had specifically asked God not to let them die, and now they were both gone, much too soon. But during the four years between my parents' deaths, God brought me to the place of being able to trust Him. The morning of my father's death, I was sitting on the edge of the bed, and God was clearly speaking to my heart, "André, even though I have used your mother and father to provide for you and take care of you through the years, I am your provider and protector." At that moment, I understood that all those years of praying (including praying for my parents' protection) drew me closer to God. I cannot explain it in words, but I had an immediate sense of peace that God would provide for me and protect me. I understood that I was safe in the loving arms of my Heavenly Father. I was able to say to God, "I still don't understand why my mother died, and I don't understand why my dad just died, but I trust You. I trust You."

That doesn't mean it's easy to handle a loss. My parents have been dead for over three decades, and I still cry sometimes. When I watch my children achieve something, I think about my birth parents and how they are missing these special times. Then I remember that they very well may be able to experience these good times from a heavenly perspective. When you come to the place of saying, "God, I still trust you. I do not understand it, but I trust you," it will change your life. It will absolutely free you. Whether God allows something that you perceive to be good to come into your life or whether He allows what you perceive to be bad to come into your life, you can trust that He is God and, therefore, that He is in control.

Prayer Is Passive, or Is It?

A lot of people either give up on prayer or tuck it in the back of some spiritual closet because it's not very exciting. Why pray for a miracle when you can go out and make things happen yourself? Most of us prefer to *do* something when we are faced with a challenge, and prayer feels like we're just sitting around waiting for something to happen. A lot of us are like Larry the Cable Guy, whose philosophy is "Git-R-Done!"

When I announce the need for some men and women to help with a work project at the church, usually plenty of people show up, on time and ready to go to work. When the sign-up sheet for mission trips goes around, it gets filled quickly. Most Christians love to roll up their sleeves and get a little dirt under their fingernails for Jesus — for that I am extremely grateful. But try to get people to show up "just to pray," and the results are often disappointing.

I'm not one to regularly hearken back to the good old days, because much about them wasn't as good as we remember it. But churches used to put more focus on prayer. Members would gather for prayer meetings, during which basically all they did was pray. Often on their knees! In 1987 I had the distinct blessing of traveling to Seoul, South Korea, to participate in an evangelistic campaign. My friend and mentor Dickson Rial, who led the trip, tried to prepare me for what I would encounter, but I'm not sure anything could have prepared me for what I found: a church that truly understood what it means to pray. The members of the church had prayed faithfully for months prior to our team's arrival. They had participated in prayer meetings that often went on for hours and sometimes all night long. Every person on our team had been bathed in prayer, as had every person we were scheduled to go with to witness and those with whom we were going to share Christ.

I am embarrassed to say that in all of my years of attending church in the United States, and even serving as a pastor, I had never encountered the awesome work of God so uniquely tied to prayer. These precious believers were committed to remaining in constant contact with their Heavenly Father, and it inspired me to revitalize my own prayer life. The church in which we were ministering had around five thousand active members at the time, and the vast majority of them were faithfully involved in prayer as a way of life. To them, prayer is anything but passive; God uses it to get things done.

I have a friend in his midfifties who confessed that often when he tries to pray, he falls asleep. I'm guessing he needs to get to bed a little earlier, but a lot of people have expressed a similar sense that prayer isn't exactly a contact sport. I know what they mean, which is why I will be introducing you to a new way to pray, one that indeed involves contact. But first, I'd like to challenge this idea that prayer is passive, even a little boring. Imagine being hired in at a minimum-wage job in the largest multinational corporation in the world. You don't have a title. You don't have anyone reporting to you. You're lucky if your supervisor even knows your name. But before the end of your first day on the job, you get a memo from the CEO, whose corner office is on the top floor of the world's tallest building halfway around the globe from your little cubicle. And that memo, addressed to you personally, says, "Welcome to the company. Here's my personal cell phone number. I'd love to hear from you as often as you can find time to talk with me."

That's just a tiny comparison of what prayer is for Christians. The Creator of the universe, the God of Abraham and David, the Father of our Lord, has invited you to do the same thing. I've heard people say, "When I get to heaven, I've got a lot of questions for God." Why not ask Him now? If prayer is passive and boring, it's because we make it that way. If you're angry at God, let Him know. He can take it. If you don't understand why He hasn't given you that promotion, tell Him. Laugh with Him about the way you keep losing your car keys and always ask Him to help you find them. Cry on His shoulder when the pain of a daughter's poor decisions is just too much to bear. Prayer should be anything but listless utterances of "help me with this" or "please take care of that." It's our opportunity to speak directly with God about anything. There are no rules or limitations, just an open invitation to "bring it."

If you still think prayer is passive or boring, check out websites like *www.24-7prayer.com* or *www.letterstoGodthemovie.com*. People from all over the world are using the internet to build a massive movement of Christians committed to praying every day.

Prayer Requires Discipline

Have you ever tried to start a good habit? It happens every January. You decide to join a health club and start exercising. Or read three chapters of the Bible every day. Or spend time in private prayer every day.

So how consistent are you with your new good habit come February? Ouch!

I'm convinced that most people *want* to pray and know they *should* pray, and they periodically commit to setting aside time each day to have a conversation with God. But soon it becomes one of those many good things we know we should do but just don't have the discipline to continue.

I read once that for anything to become habitual, you have to do it for at least forty days. So one answer to the discipline issue is to set a goal to pray every day for forty days. But maybe a better approach is not to make prayer seem like such a difficult thing that it takes such huge discipline. While I think it's great to establish a set time and maybe even a particular place to pray every day, prayer won't seem like such a burden if you give yourself permission to vary your schedule. For example, if you've committed to praying for ten minutes in the morning before you go to work, and you wake up late and have to rush to your job and miss your prayer time, you didn't fail. You have the rest of the day to pray—perhaps during your lunch break, when you get home from work, or before you go to bed.

Just Pray

In the following chapters, I will introduce an approach to prayer that will revitalize your prayer life, but no method can make you pray. At some point, you need to recognize both your own need to pray as well as the wonderful gift that prayer is for the Christian. Prayer should never become an obligation, nor should you give up or feel discouraged when you go through dry periods when it is difficult to pray. God loves to hear from us regularly, and if we miss a few days, He's patient. So to get started, use the space below and on the following page to list as many reasons as you can for why you want to pray.

Prayer 101

He knows my name.
He knows my every thought.
He sees each tear that falls
And hears me when I call.
— Tommy Walker, "He Knows My Name"

Walk into your favorite bookstore and head for the health and fitness section, and you'll find row upon row of books about exercise, nutrition, and other aspects of healthy living. You'll probably also see several people who are trying to select just the right book to help them lose weight and get back into a size they wore ten years ago. All those books are certainly helpful, but when it comes to weight loss and better health, the answers are pretty simple. Move a little more. Eat a little less. Stay away from too much sugar and fat. Did I mention move a little more? You can have the most exotic plan and buy all the right equipment, shoes, and clothing, but the basics remain the same. More activity. Less food.

Prayer is a little like that. You can attend workshops and conferences on prayer. You can choose from hundreds of books (including this one) about prayer. You can hear sermons on prayer and consult the hundreds of Bible passages about prayer. But at the end of the day, you just have to pray. Give it a try. The lyrics at the beginning of this chapter summarize the complexity and mystery of prayer and help us understand the basics: God knows us by name and cares about us; He hears us whenever we call out to Him; we pray to Him alone and no one else. In this chapter, we will look at what prayer is, how to do it, and why it is important for the life of every Christian.

God's Gift to You

Over the last twenty-five years of being a pastor, I have found that many people seem a little frightened of praying. They especially don't like to be called on to pray in public, but they also seem afraid to pray in private because they don't know how to pray or they're afraid they'll ask for something and not get it. The truth is that prayer is one of the greatest, most wonderful gifts that God has given us. Every child of God can experience it. Simply put, prayer is the gift of being able to communicate directly, regularly, and freely with God. We do not have to go through anyone else. We can do it whenever and wherever we want. And it does not cost us anything.

Prayer is not something we impose on God but rather a conversation He invites us to have with Him, one that promises results: "Call to me and I will answer you and tell you great and unsearchable things you do not know" (Jer. 33:3). God's Word is true; you can rely on it without hesitation. When you pray to the one true God, you do not have to wonder if He hears you; you can pray confidently, knowing that He not only hears you but *will* answer you.

Do you remember ever calling out from your bedroom for your mother or father to come to your bedside? It was dark, and maybe a storm had frightened you, or maybe you had a bad dream. When you called out to them, you *knew* they would respond. You could count on one or both of them being at your side within seconds because they loved you and wanted to comfort you. That's exactly what we can expect when we pray. God is always there; He's at your side the minute you call out to Him. Think about that for a moment. You have an instant connection to God. You can talk to Him anytime and know that He hears you.

God has given us the wonderful privilege of experiencing His presence in prayer, but He does not stop there. He also promises to listen to us and actually *answer* our prayers. Some have said that Jeremiah 33:3 is God's phone number: "Call to me and I will answer." Earlier in the book of Jeremiah, God gives us this promise: " 'For I know the plans I have for you,' declares the LORD, 'plans to prosper you and not to harm you, plans to give you hope and a future. Then you will call upon me and come and pray to me, and I will listen to you' " (Jer. 29:11 – 12). In the New Testament, Jesus teaches that "if you believe, you will receive whatever you ask for in prayer" (Matt. 21:22).

To participate in this great gift of prayer that God has given us, we are required to do two things: call and believe. God said, "I have great plans for you; I have wonderful plans for you!" Before we can realize those plans, however, we must first call Him and spend time with Him. Why? Because God wants to have a relationship with us. He didn't have to do it this way. God can do whatever He wants. He could have made prayer an automatic process whereby He just looks into our minds, knows what we need, and then delivers it to us. But He didn't do that because He loves to hear from us; He loves to connect with us through prayer.

The second requirement is that we must believe, and that's where many of us run into trouble. I'm convinced a lot of people pray because it seems like the appropriate thing to do, but they don't really believe it will accomplish anything. It's almost a cultural thing: the phrases "Our prayers are with the victims" and "I'll say a prayer for you" have become standard responses, but do we really believe that prayer makes a difference? God expects us to believe when we talk to Him. Imagine what it must be like from His perspective. His children ask Him for things without believing that He can deliver. If we pray without believing, we are insulting God.

Whenever we find it difficult to believe something, we turn to faith. Faith is that inner conviction that helps us believe the unbelievable. There have been times when my beloved Tennessee Titans faced an opponent so strong that it appeared obvious to everyone that the Titans couldn't possibly win. All the evidence pointed to a sure defeat, but that didn't stop me from watching the game and cheering for my team. While it was hard for most to *believe* that they would win, I had *faith* that they would. My faith in them was so strong that I expected an upset. And even if they were behind by seven points with the clock winding down, I still had faith that someone on the defense would intercept a pass and run it back for a touchdown, and then we would win on a two-point conversion. Let me tell you, that's faith!

Now if I can summon that kind of faith for a football team, shouldn't I be able to have faith in a God who has promised to listen to my prayers and act on them? The next time you pray, try beginning with these words: "I confess that I have difficulty believing that You are listening to me, but I am choosing to have faith that You are and that You will answer me."

The Mechanics of Prayer

So how do you actually pray? If prayer is a conversation based on a relationship with God, then praying is as simple as talking to a friend. Some people shy away from praying because they think they have to use religious words and act stiff and formal. Would you talk that way to a friend? As we will learn in chapter 5, God actually warns us against trying to sound religious when we pray. Then He offers specific instructions on how to pray by giving us what has become known as the Lord's Prayer: "Our Father in heaven, hallowed be your name, your kingdom come, your will be done on earth as it is in heaven. Give us today our daily bread. Forgive us our debts, as we also have forgiven our debtors. And lead us not into temptation, but deliver us from the evil one" (Matt. 6:9–13).

What we learn from this model prayer is that first we call out to God ("Our Father in heaven"). You might say "Dear God" or "Dear Heavenly Father." The words aren't as important as the fact that you are calling Him by name. In some religions, followers are required to bang on a drum or a bell to get their god's attention. Sadly, those poor people can bang on their drums all day and it won't matter. No one's home. God, however, not only is very much alive and active throughout the entire world; He answers whenever we call Him.

The Lord's Prayer also demonstrates an attitude of respect that we should have when we come before God ("hallowed be your name"). When you talk to God, honor Him with your praise. Thank Him for who He is and for what He is doing. This is as much for your own sake as it is for His; you are reminding yourself who you're talking to and what He has done for you.

The final aspect of this model prayer is what most of us think of when we think of prayer: asking for help. The prayer asks for sustenance ("daily bread"), forgiveness, and protection. God invites us to ask for anything. He cares about your physical well-being, your work, your family and friends. More than anything, He cares about your spiritual life, so He welcomes confession and repentance of anything in your life that displeases Him and readily offers forgiveness.

I would add only one other component to your prayer, one that is mentioned in the gospel of John: "And I will do whatever you ask in my name" (John 14:13). This promise from God is worthy of our attention because it reminds us of the power that is present in the name of Jesus: "Therefore God exalted him to the highest place and gave him the name that is above every name, that at the name of Jesus every knee should bow" (Phil. 2:9–10). Increasingly, people are being led to believe that there are many paths to God, but the Bible makes it clear that there is only one path to God, and that is through Jesus. It is for this reason that we should always pray, "In Jesus' name."

While I believe God listens to us regardless of how we speak to Him, this model prayer, along with the promise from John's gospel, can serve as a template for you if you are new to prayer or find it difficult to pray. In everyday language, it might sound something like this: "Dear God, You are so great. Thank you for all the good things in my life. Please help me do my job well today. Protect my children while they are in school. Encourage my husband, because he is so worried about his job and our finances. I'm asking for these things in Jesus' name, amen."

Where did the "amen" come from? It's an interesting word that Christians use all the time, but most probably don't know exactly what it means or why they use it, only that every prayer they've heard ends that way. In a way, it's kind of like officially signing off or saying goodbye at the end of a conversation. But it's more than that. The word *amen* traces its roots all the way back to the Old Testament where, in the Hebrew language, it means "certainty" or "truth." Its usage has come to mean "so be it" or "we all agree on this as truth." So ending your prayer with the word *amen* is basically saying, "This prayer is true, and God and I agree with it." There's no magic in the word *amen*; it's simply a reminder that prayer is not just words spoken into thin air but rather an honest, heartfelt conversation with God.

When is the best time to have a conversation with God? And do we need to designate a special place for prayer? The great thing about prayer is that you can pray anytime and anywhere. You can pray on your morning commute, whether you're in your car or on a bus. You can pray in the kitchen while you're making lunches for your kids, and you can pray at your desk before going into an important meeting. The apostle Paul encourages us to "pray continually" (1 Thess. 5:17), meaning we should have a constant attitude of prayer, turning to God throughout the day.

Most people, however, do find it helpful to set aside a regular time and place for prayer. The time you choose will depend on your particular rhythms. If you're a morning person, for example, you would probably have your prayer time in the morning. To avoid interruptions or distractions, you might also want to find a quiet place to have your conversation with God. In His Sermon on the Mount, Jesus offers this advice: "When you pray, go into your room, close the door and pray to your Father, who is unseen" (Matt. 6:6). Susanna Wesley, the mother of the great eighteenth-century preacher John Wesley (and eighteen other children!) was said to have sat in a chair with her apron over her head when she prayed, signaling to her busy household that they had better not interrupt her. Living in a parsonage with nineteen kids, she obviously didn't have a spare room.

Establishing a special place makes it more likely that you'll actually spend time alone with God. It could be on your porch or deck, out in the yard somewhere, a place at your office, in your car, or anywhere you can be alone and not be distracted. I often pray while I'm driving. If you have a long commute to work, you may want to try that too, but be sure to turn the radio or CD player off. And don't close your eyes!

By the way, Mrs. Wesley prayed at least an hour a day. It is reported that her son John spent several hours in prayer every day, usually early in the morning or late in the evening. You may have heard similar stories about people who spend great amounts of time in prayer, and you decided that this prayer thing isn't for you; you just don't have that kind of time. While I am grateful for stories of such "prayer warriors," it can be a little intimidating to think of praying for an hour or more each day. If you are just beginning to try to establish the practice of praying every day, don't pay much attention to time. If your conversation with God takes only a few minutes, that's fine. It's far better to do that every day than to avoid prayer because you think you have to spend an hour on your knees. It's not the length of our prayers that matters; it's our desire to spend time regularly with God.

Sharing the Gift

One of the greatest gifts we can give to our children or grandchildren is to teach them how to pray. Depending on their ages, you can sit down with them and explain how they can talk to God every day. If you attend a church that provides Sunday school or some other small-group ministry, they will also learn about prayer from their teachers. And at your Christian bookstore, you can find many wonderful, age-appropriate books that will help you teach your children or grandchildren how to pray. But the best way to teach them about prayer is to model it for them. Kids learn so much from us by watching and imitating us. So if you want them to learn how to pray, make sure they see you praying. One suggestion is to say a prayer or a blessing before each meal. Pray with them at night before they go to bed. If they see you praying alone in your den or at the kitchen table, prayer will seem natural to them. Some families try to have either a daily or weekly time of family devotions, when they gather to read from the Bible or a Bible storybook and pray as a family. Not only is this a wonderful practice that keeps families close to each other and to God; it's also a great opportunity to teach your children how to pray. I cherish the time Sarah and I spend each night with our children, having our family prayer and worship time.

Finally, if you are married, it's important to share the gift of prayer with your spouse. As much as possible, try to find time each day to pray together as a couple. There's something about praying with my wife that draws me closer to her, and as parents, we use this time to pray for our children and for each other. If you've never done it, try it. It's truly a humbling and blessed experience to hear your spouse pray for you by name.

Keep Practicing Prayer

To be perfectly honest, some of the best prayers I have ever heard are the prayers of new Christians who don't know how to pray. They use all the "wrong" words and often stop and start because they don't know what to say next. But they just open their hearts to God and blurt out their praises and their needs without pretense. Honest prayers that reflect what's really going on in our lives are the prayers God loves to hear.

As you make prayer a regular practice, you will find yourself spending more time praying and listening. You will learn that God cares about every area of your life, and you will feel more and more comfortable opening your heart to Him. Please don't spend too much time worrying about impressing God (or anyone else) with your prayers. The great South African writer and pastor Andrew Murray once wrote, "Some people pray just to pray and some people pray to know God." When you talk to God openly and honestly, as you would talk to your best friend, you will get to know Him better.

Heavenly Correspondence

When was the last time you got a letter in the mail? Not a bill or junk mail but a real handwritten letter addressed specifically to you from someone you know. I'm guessing it's been a while. With today's technology, fewer people write letters. Email, texting, IMing, online chatting, blogging, twittering, and other forms of social networking have made letter writing practically obsolete, which is too bad. While I truly enjoy being able to stay instantly in touch with friends and family all over the world, there's something special about opening the mailbox and seeing an envelope with your name written on it in the familiar handwriting of a loved one. As one daughter said to her dad when she was home from college during a holiday, "Daddy, could you send me some *real* mail sometime?" This from a texting phenomenon who could tap out messages to her friends while watching TV and listening to music. With all of her high-tech savvy, she knew that it is still hard to find a better and more personal way to share your heart with someone than with a handwritten note or letter.

Few things are as special and meaningful to me as receiving a letter from a trusted friend or relative. When you open your mailbox and pull out a letter addressed to you, don't you get a little excited? I mean, you were probably expecting the usual assortment of bills and junk mail, so that envelope addressed to you in familiar handwriting almost jumps out of the stack. I'll bet you open it right there and read it on the spot, and when you get back to your easy chair, you sit down and read it again.

Now think back to when you received a love letter. If today's young couples don't exchange love letters, they don't know what they're missing.

A text or email can't come close to the thrill of receiving a special envelope that has been sprinkled with cologne or perfume. Oh, how I cherished Sarah's love letters! (Still do.) I savored them because they made me feel so special, because Sarah thought enough of me to take the time and effort to reveal her inmost, passionate thoughts, and because she trusted me with the greatest gift of all: her heart.

It is the gift of your whole heart that God most desires, a heart without pretense or posturing, a heart in all its honesty, beauty, passion, and brokenness, a heart pulsing with love, joy, sadness, delight, doubt, pain, anguish, even anger. True love expresses all emotions, and true love — God's true love for you — accepts them.

I received a special surprise letter not long ago. If you had asked me to write down the names of a thousand people who might have appreciated the role I played in their lives, I never would have named the person who wrote me the letter. I had no idea I had done anything special for this person, but out of the blue, a letter appeared from him. He updated me on his family and what he was doing. He shared what God was doing in their lives, and then he ended by thanking me for what I had added to his life over the years. That letter made my day. Actually, it made my month! The appreciation expressed through that letter blessed me more than I can explain.

Letters are special, aren't they?

Patrick Doughtie wrote the screenplay for the movie *Letters to God* as a result of God's inspiring him through his little son, though the movie itself is not Tyler's real-life story. After Tyler's death, Patrick found a couple of letters Tyler had written to God, and he crafted his screenplay around the idea of a young boy keeping a running correspondence with God, writing Him letters and then putting them in the mailbox.

As we made the movie *Letters to God*, everyone involved wanted to show moviegoers what prayer is all about. We tried to demonstrate throughout the movie how naturally believers turn to God for help. We see Maddy, Tyler's mother, as she intercedes for her young son. We see Olivia, Tyler's grandmother, praying for her daughter and her two grandsons. We see Ben, Tyler's older brother, praying for understanding when he is brokenhearted, disturbed, and mad at God. We discover that Tyler's church family is regularly praying for him too (which happened in real life at our church). And we see how Brady, the mail carrier, a troubled alcoholic, gives his heart to God and follows Tyler's example by encouraging others to pray by writing letters to God.

Although I've been a Christian since I was a teenager and have written prayers in a journal for some time, I had never thought of prayer as writing letters to God. But when I learned about Tyler's letters, it made perfect sense. After all, prayer is expressing your heart to God. Who says it always has to be done verbally? And when you stop to think about it, many of the psalms are written prayers to God. As I began writing out my prayers to God in the form of letters, it opened up a new dimension to my prayer life.

Why Write?

At least three benefits of writing my prayers stand out. You might find this hard to believe about a preacher (although we are just like everyone else), but when I pray, I sometimes get distracted. I guess it happens to all of us. I get away by myself every day to pray, and I thoroughly depend on the time I spend with God. But every now and then, usually when I have a lot of things going on in my life, my mind wanders. I've discovered that writing out my prayers keeps me focused. The act of putting pen to paper forces me to think about what I want to say and keeps my attention directed toward God.

I've also found that writing letters to God infuses my prayer life with a little variety. Have you ever felt like you're in a rut when it comes to praying? Often we settle into a routine of basically praying for the same things, using the same words, until prayer becomes almost a lifeless ritual. Writing my prayers breaks up the routine because I can't rely on the same old words and phrases. The blank sheet of paper in front of me is an invitation to try something new. It also leads me to think about what I want to say to God rather than leaving my mind on autopilot and racing to the "amen."

Finally, writing letters to God gives me a record of my prayers, which produces two additional benefits. First, you learn a lot about yourself and your relationship with God when you go back and read your prayers. Second, you see how God has responded to your prayers. For example, I have written prayers in which I asked God to help me lead a specific individual into a relationship with Him. Imagine how thrilling and encouraging it is to read that prayer several months later, knowing that this person for whom you prayed has been transformed through God's gift of salvation.

Recently I began working with a young man who struggled with addictions to drugs and alcohol and wanted to turn his life around. We began meeting, and I have to say his honesty in dealing with his struggle was so refreshing to me. So many people wear a mask and try to put on a show of religiosity when they're around their pastor, but this guy didn't hold anything back as he shared his journey with me. He received Jesus as his Lord and Savior and seemed to be making a lot of progress until one day, in his typical straightforward manner, he told me he had "messed up" and felt he needed to get some professional help. He asked if we could pray together, and I assured him that we could, but I took it one step farther: "I'd like you to write down what you'd like to say to God." I'm not saying a verbal prayer wouldn't have been sufficient, but his written prayer gave him a reference point as he continued dealing with his struggles, and I knew having it with him would give him the courage to stick with the process.

The Act of Writing

You don't have to be a professional writer to write your prayers to God. At first, it may seem awkward or even a bit difficult to write down your prayers. Some of us still have nightmares about having to write essays in English classes and then getting them back with the teacher's critical comments in red ink bleeding all over our hard work. No one, least of all God, is going to give you a grade on how well you write these letters. If you can write a note to your wife, jot down a list of things to pick up at the store, or scribble instructions for the neighbor who will be caring for your pet while you're on vacation, you can write a letter to God.

I encourage you to keep your written prayers in a way that will allow you to occasionally go back and read them and reflect on how God has responded to them. Any old notebook or binder will do, but I know many people use journals, which are readily available in bookstores. They tend to be more permanent, preserving your writing, and they are easily stored on a bookshelf. They come in a variety of sizes, including smaller ones that you can easily carry in your purse or your pocket.

I also recommend that you try to set aside a specific time for writing your letters to God, perhaps making it part of your daily devotions. If you've never practiced daily devotions, now's a good time to start. One of the best ways to maintain a relationship with God and thus grow in your faith is to spend time with Him each day, praying to Him, reading His Word—the Bible—and then meditating on it and listening to what He is saying to you. God seldom speaks to us in an audible voice but rather directs our thoughts to what He wants us to do. "Instead of shouting, He whispers," writes Margaret Feinberg in *God Whispers*. If you pay attention with a quiet and open heart, you will hear those whispers in the thoughts and ideas that God gives you.

Start slowly until you become more comfortable writing your prayers. Instead of trying to write a prayer every day, begin by writing one a week. Then throughout the rest of the week, read that written prayer out loud as part of your prayer time. You may want to add more "writing days" to your devotions, but if you write only one prayer a week, that is fine. Imagine, at the

LIGHTHOUSE
7188 AMADOR PLAZA RD.
DUBLIN, CA 94568 925-829-3698
WWW.DUBLINLIGHTHOUSE.COM

1 Dept 06

GIFTS

Sub Total	1.39
Sales Tax	.12
Total Due	1.51
Cash Paid	1.51

Change   .00

This Transaction # 1212795

NOV 1, 2011 10:32 1 - SH 01

THANK YOU!

CATHERINE IGNACIO

RETURN POLICY - ALL ITEMS EXCEPT
CLEARANCE ITEMS CAN BE
RETURNED WITH A RECEIPT WITHIN 30 DAYS
FROM DATE OF PURCHASE. ANY PURCHASE MADE
WITH A CHECK MUST WAIT 2 WEEKS BEFORE
CASH WILL BE GIVEN BACK BUT CAN BE
EXCHANGED IMMEDIATELY.

end of a year, you would have fifty-two written prayers in your journal. The goal here isn't quantity but an added dimension of quality to your prayer life.

Most letters begin with a salutation, which simply is addressing the person to whom you're writing. Little Tyler began his letters, "Dear God," and that works for me because it reminds me that this isn't just an ordinary letter to an earthly friend. You may want to vary the way you start your letters to God, but I think it's important to begin just as you would with any letter: "Hi God," "Hey God," "Good morning, Lord," and so on. Personally, I'm uncomfortable being too informal with God when I address Him, but I'm sure God doesn't really mind a shout-out like, "What's up, God?" if it makes prayer easier for you and if you are sincere and respectful when you do it. Jesus even said we can simply call God Daddy.

Finally, put a date on your prayers, just as you would any other letter. This will be helpful when you look back over your prayer journal. Your written prayers will become a record of your spiritual journey with God.

What do you write? Whatever is on your heart. In the words of William Wordsworth, "Fill your paper with the breathings of your heart." Focus on God and share your heart with Him. God is big enough for you to be honest with Him. There's no right or wrong way to pray. Some people like to use the acronym ACTS: adoration (praising God), confession (telling Him the things you have done wrong and for which you are sorry), thanksgiving (thanking Him for the good in your life), supplication (asking Him to address your need or the need of someone else). The most important thing to remember as you write your prayer is that it should come from your heart. What would you like to say to God? What would you like Him to do? What burden do you want to share with Him? Write it in your letter to God and then "send" it with the closing, "In Jesus' name, amen."

Getting Started

Have you ever been deeply in love with someone? I have, and I still am, with my wife, Sarah. If I ever have to be out of town without her, one of the first things I do when I get cell-phone service is call her. I have a deep desire to talk with her. One of the keys to a more vibrant prayer life is a similar deep desire to talk with God. Desire is a funny thing; you know whether you have it by what you do. If someone has a deep desire to do something, they usually end up doing it if they are at all able to do so. If you have a passionate desire for sewing, you will find a way to sew. If you have a passionate desire for golfing, you will find a way to golf. When the desire is present, everything else will take care of itself. For example, I love to watch football games. I still have the desire to play football, but I no longer have the physical ability to do so. (Some would argue that I never had it in the first place.) You don't have to ask me to set aside time on weekends to watch a football game, especially if it's a game involving one of my favorite teams. I already know what time the game is scheduled to begin, and I am ready to enjoy it from the opening kickoff. And the more football I watch, the more football I want to watch. That is how Christians should think of prayer. While football is a passion of mine, my life doesn't depend on my watching football games. But the growth of our spiritual lives — our relationship with Jesus — does depend on our spending time with Him regularly in prayer. Instead of thinking about your desire to pray, then, think more about your desire to have a dynamic relationship with God. Do you want to please Him? Do you want to grow in your faith? Do you want to make a difference in the world? Do you want to have a stronger spiritual influence on your family? When you focus more on your relationship with God, you will develop a stronger desire to pray. Writing your prayers will simply add a new dimension to your relationship with God and, at least for me, create an even stronger desire to continue writing letters to God.

In addition to keeping our focus on why we want to pray, we need to make prayer a priority. Again, Jesus' example is helpful. As we read about His life in the Gospels, one thing is clear: people constantly clamored for His time. They gathered to hear Him speak, and perfect strangers approached Him to ask for healing. In one account, a group of men climbed up on the roof of a house to lower a man down to where Jesus was, hoping He would heal their friend. We also see Him getting away from the crowds to talk with His Father, and that's because He knew how important that regular communication was to successfully carrying out His mission on earth. Busyness is not an excuse for not praying. My schedule can get pretty hectic, but somehow I always find the time to watch football. In a much more significant way, because I know how much I need to be and desire to be in communion with God, I choose to make prayer a priority of my life. I have learned that if I don't set my schedule, someone else will. I know the importance of blocking off time early in the morning to ensure that I will be able to spend time with God, because if I don't protect that time, I will have no problem filling it with other good activities. Prayer, however, is the fuel that enables us to do all those good things better.

Learning to Pray from Jesus

As Christians, we are literally "followers of Christ." So when it comes to prayer, the best thing we can do is follow His example. Before we move on to the actual practice of writing prayers as letters to God, let's take a look at how Jesus prayed and see what we can learn from it. In the space provided following each Scripture passage, write what God is teaching you about the role of prayer in Jesus' life and how you can apply that to your own prayer life. To help you get started, I've included my thoughts for the first passage.

Matthew 6:5–8

And when you pray, do not be like the hypocrites, for they love to pray standing in the synagogues and on the street corners to be seen by men. I tell you the truth, they have received their reward in full. But when you pray, go into your room, close the door and pray to your Father, who is unseen. Then your Father, who sees what is done in secret, will reward you. And when you pray, do not keep on babbling like pagans, for they think they will be heard because of their many words. Do not be like them, for your Father knows what you need before you ask him.

Jesus is teaching me to be careful whenever I pray in front of other people. I should pray the same way in church or in small groups as I do in private. He also seems to be saying to keep my prayers short. My desire should be to impress God, not people. Longer prayers do not equal better prayers. God is much more concerned with my heart.

Matthew 14:22–23

Immediately Jesus made His disciples get into the boat and go before Him to the other side, while He sent the multitudes away. And when He had sent the multitudes away, He went up on the mountain by Himself to pray. Now when evening came, He was alone there. (NKJV)

Matthew 26:39, 42, 44

Going a little farther, he fell with his face to the ground and prayed, "My Father, if it is possible, may this cup be taken from me. Yet not as I will, but as you will." He went away a second time and prayed, "My Father, if it is not possible for this cup to be taken away unless I drink it, may your will be done." So he left them and went away once more and prayed the third time, saying the same thing.

Mark 1:35

And in the morning, rising up a great while before day, he went out, and departed into a solitary place, and there prayed. (KJV)

Luke 11:9–10

So I say to you: Ask and it will be given to you; seek and you will find; knock and the door will be opened to you. For everyone who asks receives; he who seeks finds; and to him who knocks, the door will be opened.

Preparing Your Heart for Prayer

I mentioned earlier that practically everyone has said some sort of prayer at least once in their lives. Chances are, many of them were disappointed with the results: "I lost my job, the bank was about to foreclose on our home, and I couldn't afford to even buy Christmas presents for my kids, so I said a prayer and bought a lottery ticket, and guess what? The Big Guy didn't come through!"

True prayer is fellowship and communication with God, not a magic wand we can wave and get whatever we want. To enjoy that fellowship, we need to have a relationship with Him. Would you walk up to a stranger in the grocery store and begin a deep conversation with her? Yet that's how many people approach prayer. We get real earnest about it when we are in trouble or have a pressing need, but the rest of the time we tend to go it alone. We rob ourselves of the power of prayer if we do not have a close relationship with God.

If you aren't sure what it means to have a personal relationship with God, the Bible is quite clear about it, and it is actually quite simple: believe. "Believe in the Lord Jesus, and you will be saved" (Acts 16:31). That's all it takes to become a Christian. You must believe that Jesus is the Son of God, who died to pay for your sins, was buried, and rose again, and your belief must lead you to receiving Jesus as your Lord and Savior. You may have gotten the impression from church folk that you have to *do* a lot of things, or *quit* doing a lot of things, to become a Christian. Even the religious leaders in Jesus' day thought that and asked Him what works they had to do to become His followers. His answer? "The work of God is this: to believe in the one he has sent"

(John 6:29). To these religious people who had been taught that being good enough for God meant they could eat only certain foods and wear certain clothes, this seemed too easy. So they kept asking about the requirements to join those people who eventually became known as Christians. "I tell you the truth," Jesus answered, "he who believes has everlasting life" (John 6:47).

You might find it difficult to believe in something as supernatural as the idea of Jesus' being the Son of God, and that's okay. Sincere belief is more than words. It must come from the heart, and in our rationalistic age, people often have difficulty believing what they cannot see. That was true in Jesus' day also. A man who wanted Jesus to heal his son approached Him and humbly asked, "If you can do anything, take pity on us and help us." Jesus repeated, "'If you can'?" Then He said, "Everything is possible for him who believes." In simple honesty, the man replied, "I do believe; help me overcome my unbelief!" (Mark 9:22–24).

The man's response was enough for Jesus. He healed the man's son.

Maybe your belief is like that man's. You *want* to believe, but you also have a lot of questions. That's enough for Jesus. If you say, "Lord, I believe; help me when I have doubts," and if your belief leads you to repent of your sin and receive Jesus as your Savior and Lord, you have begun a relationship with God that will deepen as you regularly meet Him in prayer.

Prayer Barriers

While having a relationship with God makes it possible to have a dynamic prayer life, it doesn't guarantee one. God always listens to the cries of His children, but He is less likely to take us seriously if we don't take Him seriously. Some of us are like the school kid who is a terror in the classroom yet can't understand why the teacher never lets him go to the front of the lunch line or enjoy other classroom privileges. Certain things can hinder our prayer life, and most have to do with our attitude when we approach God in prayer. As author Bingham Hunter wrote in *The God Who Hears*, "God does not just hear your prayers. He hears your whole life. He does not respond to what you say. He responds to what you are. He responds to you."[1] If your heart isn't right, you most likely will find yourself just going through the motions of prayer.

Before we look at things that can get in the way of a dynamic prayer life, let's make something very clear: God is sovereign—meaning He is totally in control of all creation—and He can answer any prayer He chooses to answer. There are no formulas to guarantee that your prayers will be answered the way you desire, and if you're looking for the right way to pray to ensure you will get everything you ask for, you won't find it here. At the same time, the Bible offers some clear guidance about how we should pray.

Scripture teaches us that several things can hinder a dynamic prayer life. The first barrier to prayer is an unforgiving heart. For example, don't try praying for some great need if you're carrying a grudge against someone; it won't work. If you try to pray yet you have not forgiven those who have wronged you, your prayers will seem hollow because, in your heart, you know that God expects you to forgive others just as He has forgiven you: "Be kind and compassionate to one another, forgiving each other, just as in Christ God forgave you" (Eph. 4:32). When you are unforgiving, you are not demonstrating the heart of God. Jesus said, "When you stand praying, if you hold anything against anyone, forgive him, so that your Father in heaven may forgive you your sins" (Mark 11:25). When you refuse to forgive others, a barrier develops between you and God.

The second barrier to prayer could be that pedestal you're proudly standing on. By its very nature, prayer is a humbling experience. You, a mere mortal, are approaching the Almighty. There's no place for arrogance or pride when it comes to prayer. Jesus often taught by telling stories, and, in a story about a religious leader and a tax collector, He taught us how a prideful attitude can undermine our prayers. Both men went to church to pray, and the religious leader stood up in front of the synagogue so everyone could see him and prayed out loud, "God, I thank you that I am not like other men — robbers, evildoers, adulterers — or even like this tax collector." Keep in mind that tax collectors were universally hated in those days. But this tax collector, Jesus said, stayed at the back of the synagogue and looked down at his feet and quietly said, "God, have mercy on me, a sinner." Jesus ended the story with this lesson for us: it was the tax collector who pleased God the most, "For everyone who exalts himself will be humbled, and he who humbles himself will be exalted" (Luke 18:11 – 14).

Arrogance is a funny thing. We easily see it in others but miss it when we look at ourselves. It doesn't help that our culture of individualism encourages us to think pretty highly of ourselves, and Christians aren't immune from this focus on self. Just as religious people in Jesus' day often acted as if they were better than others, people who regularly go to church are sometimes guilty of looking down their noses on those who don't regularly go to church. This attitude makes it difficult to have a close relationship with God, and we can't expect Him to answer our prayers if we approach Him this way. God wants us to live humbly, and He promises that when we do, He will provide the direction needed. "He guides the humble in what is right and teaches them his way" (Ps. 25:9). Whenever you pause to pray, remember who God is and who you are. Approach Him boldly, because He has invited you, but also humbly, because in His eyes you are no better than anyone else.

Some Scripture passages appear to promise that God will give us whatever we ask for.

Ask and it will be given to you.

—Matthew 7:7

For everyone who asks receives.

—Matthew 7:8

Whatever you ask for in prayer, believe that you have received it, and it will be yours.

—Mark 11:24

We certainly don't always get what we pray for, so what's going on here? Part of the answer has to do with the third barrier to prayer: wrong motives. The Bible explains, "When you ask, you do not receive, because you ask with wrong motives, that you may spend what you get on your pleasures" (James 4:3). An older man once explained that he is so glad God didn't answer all of his prayers when he was younger. "I wanted to be a professional athlete, so before every Little League game, I would be on my knees praying that I would hit home runs. I was pretty good but not good enough to make it in the pros, and looking back, I can see that what I really wanted was money and fame. God was smart enough not to give it to me."

God looks at our hearts and knows what we are really asking for when we pray. I read about a man who was taught to pray first with his hands in front of him, palms facing the ground to signify that he is emptying himself of any wrong motives and then turn his hands palms up to indicate he is willing to receive whatever God gives him in answer to his prayers. What a graphic reminder that when we pray, our motives must be pure.

Live Like You Pray, Pray Like You Live

How many friends from high school are you still close to? If you're like most of us, not very many. Yet when you were walking the halls of your old school, going to football games, and hanging out in each others' homes, you probably thought you'd all be that close for the rest of your lives. By the time you're in your forties, however, you can barely remember the names of many of your old friends, not because you're getting senile but because they sort of dropped out of your life. What happened? Did you have a falling out or deliberately erase them from your social circle? More likely, you're no longer close to your high school friends because you just drifted apart. You spent less time together. Despite good intentions, you seldom kept in touch with phone calls or letters. And now you have a family and a career, and you're just too busy to keep in touch with those old high school friends.

The same thing can happen with our relationship with God, and drifting away from Him is the fourth barrier to prayer. The wonderful old English hymn "Abide with Me" underscores the need to maintain a close relationship with God if we want to experience a rich and powerful prayer life. The third stanza begins, "I need thy presence every passing hour." Too many of us see prayer as the only time we are with God, but He expects us to be with Him all the time, to remain close by His side. Just as a branch must remain connected to the life-giving vine, so too must we remain connected to Jesus. We can get to know God better by spending time with Him every day in prayer and by reading the Bible, God's very Word. When we meet with God regularly and read and live according to His Word, we stay in fellowship with Him. Jesus put it this way: "If you remain in me and my words remain in you, ask whatever you wish, and it will be given you" (John 15:7). You cannot expect your prayers to be answered if you are trying to live your life without God. The only solution is to remain as closely connected to Him as possible, and in doing so, your prayers will be unhindered.

Unconfessed sin is the fifth barrier to a dynamic prayer life. The psalmist wrote, "If I had cherished sin in my heart, the Lord would not have listened" (Ps. 66:18). It is not that God is unable to listen to us when we sin; rather, He chooses not to listen when we have unconfessed sin and when we are unrepentant. Sin is an affront to God. It is because of our sin that God sent Jesus to die for us. Sin we haven't confessed and repented of will destroy our prayer life. Do you remember ever secretly doing something your parents had forbidden you to do? Do you remember how guilty you felt and how difficult it was for you even to look into your mom's or dad's eyes? But once you got caught and it was all out in the open, you were so relieved because you knew there was nothing between you and your parents. When we try to pray knowing that we've disappointed God by disobeying His laws, we can barely bring ourselves to mumble anything to Him. Like any good father, God wants to forgive His children, to wipe the slate clean. For Him to do that, however, we must come to Him with an open heart, confessing our sin and demonstrating our dependence on Him and His grace. John the apostle said, "If we confess our sins, he is faithful and just and will forgive us our sins and purify us from all unrighteousness" (1 John 1:9). Because of this promise, you can *always* approach God with a pure heart, and that will make a huge difference in your prayer life.

Trying to show off when we pray is the sixth barrier to prayer. You know what I'm talking about. Everyone in your small group is given an opportunity to pray out loud, and someone — never you, right? — always uses a lot of fancy words and religious language. They're not really having a conversation with anyone but instead are trying to let everyone know how religious they are. As we learned in the Scripture passages in the previous chapter, Jesus was critical of show-off praying and said it's best to pray in private so that you avoid this temptation. He didn't say it's wrong to pray in public; He just said that all of our prayers should be honest and sincere. The essence of Jesus' message on this is that we need to pray to God, not to people. Likewise, in our private prayers, we're sometimes tempted to say all the right things instead of just having an honest conversation with God. When we pray, we need to keep our focus on God and not on impressing others, ourselves, or God. Praying with hypocrisy in your heart will prevent you from praying effectively. Look deep inside your heart and make sure that, as best as you know how, you are living with a pure and transparent heart before God. When you pray, do not be concerned about what anyone but God thinks.

Have you ever been in such a hurry that you just breathe a quick prayer on the run? I have, and I think God understands. But if that becomes a habit, it will diminish my prayer life. The seventh barrier to effective prayer is lack of devotion. God doesn't do anything in a halfhearted fashion, and He doesn't want us to either. "You will seek me and find me when you seek me with all your heart," God instructs (Jer. 29:13). What does it mean to seek God "with all your heart"? I glimpsed this when I visited South Korea and saw how earnestly Christians in that country pray. Sometimes they gather and spend hours doing nothing but praying. One mountain near Seoul, the capitol of South Korea, is called Prayer Mountain. All along the mountainside, people have dugout areas where they spend entire nights praying. Korea has the highest percentage of Christians of any Asian nation, and I believe it's because years ago a small band of believers sought God with all their hearts, and now that they have grown to more than half the population, they still pray as if everything depends on it. How would *your* life be different if you prayed as if everything depends on it?

The eighth, and perhaps the biggest, barrier to an effective prayer life is lack of faith. We ask, but we don't really believe. Fortunately, Jesus doesn't expect us to have a huge reservoir of faith; He taught that even if our faith is as small as a mustard seed, it is enough to move mountains. The problem for many of us is that we don't have even that much faith. When you pray for something, do you *really* believe your prayer will be answered? This is a tough one because, as we know, not every prayer gets answered the way we want, even those prayed by stalwart prayer warriors with great faith. But why would God even listen to you if He knows you don't really believe? He knows your heart. He knows whether you are praying out of faith or just because it seems like a good thing to do. In the New Testament, James warns us about praying without faith. First, he explains that those who seek wisdom should ask God, because He "gives generously to all." Then he continues, "But when he asks, he must believe and not doubt, because he who doubts is like a wave of the sea, blown and tossed by the wind" (James 1:5–6). I will admit that having faith even the size of a tiny mustard seed is sometimes difficult, but I have found that putting my faith in God rather than in His answer keeps doubt at bay. It goes back to that word *sovereignty*. God is in charge. He knows what He is doing. His way is perfect, and if He doesn't answer my prayer exactly as I want Him to, He has a reason that I may never know. But that's okay. My faith is in Him, not in whether I get what I want. We need to pray with our faith focused on Him and trust that regardless of what happens, it is all part of His perfect will.

Finally, a special word to those of us who are husbands. According to the Bible and God's plan for families, He has designed us to be the spiritual leaders in our homes. That doesn't make us better, nor does it give us license to be controlling or domineering. Rather, it makes us responsible for nurturing a loving relationship in our marriages, and a failure to live up to this responsibility presents yet another barrier to prayer. God's Word is pretty clear on this: "Husbands, in the same way be considerate as you live with your wives, and treat them with respect as the weaker partner and as heirs with you of the gracious gift of life, so that nothing will hinder your prayers" (1 Peter 3:7). In God's perfect plan for marriage, if we do not love and honor our wives, it will not only damage our relationship with them; it will inhibit our ability to pray effectively.

God Loves to Break down Barriers

If you've ever wondered why your prayer life seems empty or why praying seldom gives you that sense of close communion with God, I hope this chapter has helped you better understand how to prepare your heart for prayer. I also hope you're not discouraged or feeling that these barriers are impossible to overcome. The same God who shattered the walls of Jericho can help you break through these barriers and lead you into His presence through effective, fervent prayer.

One word of warning, however. Even if you overcome all of these barriers to your prayer life, you may feel that your prayers are not getting through. When you don't receive what you ask for in prayer, does that mean God isn't listening or that He doesn't love you? More important, what should you do when you think God hasn't answered your prayer? We will consider this next.

Unanswered Prayers?

Few things are as discouraging to Christians as having our prayers seemingly go unanswered. I know of parents who have prayed for a prodigal child to return to faith, and it still hasn't happened. Some people in my congregation are praying to find work, but they are still unemployed. I have prayed for many things for my church and my family, but I cannot truthfully claim that God has always done as I have asked.

I remember as a child asking God for many things that I never got. I remember praying for my favorite team to win, only to watch them lose. I hate to admit it, but I have prayed that prayer as an adult too. I remember as a teenager praying that I would marry a certain girl. In God's grace, He said no, and eventually I was blessed with the best wife I ever could have hoped for. As an adult I have offered many requests to God that did not get the answer I desired. I have prayed for people to be healed who never received healing on this earth. I have prayed for people to be saved who have not yet received Jesus as their Lord and Savior. I have prayed for the marriages of friends of mine to be reconciled and strengthened, and in some cases, neither has occurred yet. I certainly know what it is like to pray and not always get the hoped-for answer.

Country singer Garth Brooks released a great song a number of years ago called "Unanswered Prayers." It really should have been called "Prayers That Had the Answer No," but I guess that doesn't sound as good as "Unanswered Prayers." The point of the song is that some of God's greatest gifts are "unanswered prayers." You prayed to marry that high school sweetheart, and when you see her twenty years later, you thank God He didn't answer your prayer the way you wanted Him to. Over the years, however, I have come to understand that the term *unanswered prayers* is misleading and contributes to a false understanding of God. If I believed that God didn't answer my prayers, I would have to believe that God either doesn't care about me or lacks the power to do what I have asked Him to do. Both of those assumptions, however, are false and go against His character. God is love; therefore, He chooses to care for you. And He is omnipotent, or all-powerful. Nothing is beyond His ability.

It may seem to you that God doesn't answer your prayers, but in reality, God always answers the prayers of His children. He just doesn't always answer them the way we want Him to. If you are a parent, you know that you can't always give your children what they ask for. Especially when our children are very young, it almost seems as if all we do is say no to their requests: "Mommy, can I have some candy?" "Daddy, can you buy me a pocketknife?" We say no because we love them and know what's best for them at the time.

We often think we know what is right and what is best in life, therefore we feel justified in praying for certain things. Then when we don't get the answer for which we were hoping, we get discouraged or angry. But as we mature spiritually, we understand that we finite humans don't always know what is best for us or our friends. We learn that God not only loves us but has a divine plan for humanity, and sometimes what we want goes against that plan.

For example, you may be familiar with the popular Christian author and speaker Joni Eareckson Tada. Her first book, *Joni*, tells the story of how a diving accident left her paralyzed from the neck down. She was only seventeen years old. By all accounts, it was a horrible tragedy, putting a young, beautiful, and active Christian woman in a wheelchair and making her dependent on others for the rest of her life. In one of her most recent books, *When God Weeps*, she tackles the mysteries of suffering and concludes that God is both wise enough to say no to our prayers and powerful enough to use those unwelcome answers for greater things than if He had said yes. Over the years, but especially in the earliest days of her injury, many people prayed for Joni's healing. Obviously, God said no, for she is still in a wheelchair. Yet her influence has been felt worldwide. Through her ministry, Joni and Friends, she has visited more than one hundred countries and has donated more than fifty thousand wheelchairs to those who were unable to afford them. Thousands have put their trust in Jesus after hearing her testimony. Her books have been translated into thirty-five languages, inspiring millions around the world. Could God have healed Joni back in 1967, when the accident occurred? He definitely could have. But in His wisdom He chose not to, knowing the greater good that would come from her service to Him, despite her being in a wheelchair.

We may think we know what's best for ourselves and others, but we have only a limited, finite perspective. We are incapable of seeing eternity as God sees it. He knows what's best for His kingdom, and it isn't always what we want.

As I mentioned earlier, the movie *Letters to God* was inspired by the life of Tyler Doughtie, a young boy from our church who was diagnosed with brain cancer. Both in the movie and in real life, many people prayed for God to heal Tyler of his cancer. The people in our church prayed for a miracle so that God would be glorified and perhaps many would come to faith after seeing this miracle. It seems like a reasonable request: "Dear God, please heal little Tyler. Don't let him suffer so. Heal him in such a way that the doctors will have to report that it was a miracle, and then many more people will believe in You."

Again, both in the movie and in real life, Tyler died. Was this unanswered prayer? Hardly. Our prayers were not answered *exactly* as we wanted them answered because God had bigger things in mind. Tyler's story continues to inspire people to turn their lives over to God. His faith in the face of cancer is the real miracle, showing others that death has no power over us if we have God in our hearts. God could have healed Tyler on this earth, but He chose not to. That doesn't mean He was absent or unloving. Throughout Tyler's struggle with cancer, God comforted him and his family, along with the rest of us who were praying for him. God's will is perfect. He does not make mistakes. He knew what He was doing when He allowed Tyler to be taken home so early in his life. We may never know the extent to which his story will touch others, but we do know this: praying for Tyler was a privilege. Of course, we wanted God to deliver what we had been praying for: Tyler's healing. Instead, we learned to trust that God's answers are always the best.

Trusting God When It Doesn't Make Sense

I'll be the first to admit that sometimes it's hard to keep praying when you don't get the answer you are looking for. I know of a man whose mother was diagnosed with Alzheimer's. At the time of the diagnosis, his mother was lucid—her old self, as he put it—about 80 percent of the time.

"But that other 20 percent was just awful," he recalls. "What hurt the most was that she didn't recognize me during those times. It was so startling to me, and the thought of her getting worse was almost more than I could bear, so I began praying every day that God would heal her. Sometimes I would lie flat on the floor of the den and cry out to God. I practiced everything I knew about prayer. I prayed in the name of Jesus and reminded God that He promised to answer any prayer that is prayed in His Son's name. I prayed boldly. I confessed any sin that might have crept into my life. I can honestly say I have never prayed so hard in my life, but she kept getting worse and then died after about two years of dementia. I have to be honest. I couldn't pray for about a year after that because I felt God let me down."

Have you ever felt that way? If so, you're not alone. A brief passage in 2 Corinthians can help us deal with this sense that God isn't listening or won't answer us, and it involves one of God's great saints: the apostle Paul. If anyone ever deserved a special pipeline to God, you would think it would have been Paul, who, once he became a believer, was an untiring and courageous missionary spreading the gospel throughout the Mediterranean region. But despite Paul's commitment to the Lord, to the onlooker it may appear as though God refused to answer one of Paul's prayers. Paul had an affliction of some kind. We don't know what it was, but his description of it has become a common expression in our language: "a thorn in my flesh" (2 Cor. 12:7). Some scholars believe it was a physical problem, perhaps a problem with his eyesight. Others think it was more spiritual in nature, a powerful temptation to sinful behavior. My own view is that God chose not to reveal the nature of this problem because He knew we would think that what Paul had to deal with is nothing compared with what we're dealing with and then ignore the teaching. Whatever it was, it's clear that the problem was serious enough for Paul to say it was sent by "a messenger of Satan, to torment me" (2 Cor. 12:7). We're talking a major, unbearable, "please get rid of this before it kills me" kind of problem. Here is Paul's description of this affliction: "To keep me from becoming conceited because of these surpassingly great revelations, there was given me a thorn in my flesh, a messenger of Satan, to torment me. Three times I pleaded with the Lord to take it away from me. But he said to me, 'My grace is sufficient for you, for my power is made perfect in weakness.' Therefore I will boast all the more gladly about my weaknesses, so that Christ's power may rest on me. That is why, for Christ's sake, I delight in weaknesses, in insults, in hardships, in persecutions, in difficulties. For when I am weak, then I am strong" (2 Cor. 12:7–10). In this brief passage, God gives us some clues about how to pray when it seems as if no one is listening.

Pray Fervently

Paul didn't just ask God to remove the problem that afflicted him so seriously; he "pleaded" with God. Words do not appear in the Bible by accident, so when Paul admits to pleading with God, he's telling us something about how to pray. It's not that pleading is more effective at getting God's attention; rather, pleading gets *our* attention. It intensifies our desire to hear from God, and if our desire to hear from Him is strong, we will be more likely to hear Him and be able to accept what He says to us.

I can recall many times when I needed God to intervene in a situation and I went to sleep crying out to Him. I prayed in earnest until sleep finally overtook me. I hoped that when I woke up in the morning the problem would be removed and everything would be perfect. The next morning would come, however, and the problem would still be with me. Was my pleading in vain? Absolutely not, because those times of crying out to God and being so vulnerable and dependent on Him drew me as close to God as I've ever been. So much of the time our prayers are tame and civil: "Dear God, please help me do Your will today. In Jesus' name, amen." We're not specific. We play it safe, making it easy to go about in our self-reliant ways. We get more worked up over politics or sports than we do about the eternal things that truly matter in life. No wonder God seems so far away when we pray so timidly. But when you pour your heart out to God in earnest, fervent prayer, it draws you close enough to Him to hear His answer. It may not be the answer you wanted, but that won't matter. Such close encounters with God shape us into who He wants us to be, regardless of life's circumstances.

Jesus' own example underscores the need to pray fervently in the face of God's apparent silence. On the night He was to be arrested, He went to the Mount of Olives to pray. Being both human and divine, Jesus knew the plan for His life, and the human side of Him was agonizing over what was about to happen. He knew He would be forced to endure the humiliation of a "kangaroo trial." He knew that He would be led through the streets of Jerusalem with a crown of thorns piercing His flesh and that He would be beaten until He could barely walk. He also knew that He would be nailed to a cross and left to die in the hot sun as His followers helplessly watched. Even more excruciating was knowing that He was about to become sin for us; the perfect Son of God was about to take our sin upon Himself. In Luke's account, as Jesus went to this quiet place to pray, He was in "anguish." He prayed so earnestly concerning what he was facing that "his sweat was like drops of blood falling to the ground" (Luke 22:44). The Son of God pleaded with His Father to spare Him from going through with the plan to save the world from sin and death by taking our sin upon Himself. I am thankful God answered Jesus' prayer the way He did, because the only hope we have is found in Jesus' becoming sin for us so that we might become the righteousness of God in

Him. It appears that while Jesus prayed so fervently, God used that time to strengthen Him to face what was ahead. He was able to hear His Father's voice say, "It's okay. I'll be with you all the way. We'll make it, and it will all be good."

If you think God isn't listening or refuses to answer your prayers, pray harder. It is in the fervency of our prayers that everything else fades away so we can hear His voice more clearly and understand His purposes better. Here are some suggestions to help you pray more fervently.

1. *Make prayer your priority.* Prayer ought to be like oxygen or food for you, something you can't live without. Look at all the things we allow to crowd our lives: watching favorite TV shows, listening to music, reading the newspaper, golfing, hunting, quilting, and so on. Nothing is wrong with these things, but would you give up time spent on these activities so that you could pray more? Do you think of prayer before you think of anything else? For too many of us, prayer is the last resort, what we turn to when everything else has failed. Corrie ten Boom once asked, "Is prayer your steering wheel or your spare tire?" Prayer becomes fervent when it is our top priority.

2. *Make prayer your passion.* If you are passionate about something, you can't wait to get to it. If you are passionate about college football, you can't wait for Saturday afternoon so you can watch it on television or, better yet, attend a game. Then during the week, you read all you can about it in the newspaper, on the internet, and anyplace else that has information about your team. Why? Because you're passionate about it. It's all-consuming. That's how we should be about prayer if we want to have a fervent prayer life. It shouldn't just be a ritual we perform during a specific time of the day; it should be something we look forward to all the time.

3. *Make prayer persistent.* The late Ruth Graham, wife of evangelist Billy Graham, experienced the pain of watching her son, Franklin, turn away from the Lord and live a life of wild rebellion. Yet she patiently and persistently prayed that Franklin would someday return to the faith he was taught and serve God. Today Franklin leads his father's evangelistic organization, along with his own Christian relief agency, and preaches the gospel all over the world. I have to believe that God used the persistent prayers of his mother to help lead Franklin back to a close walk with God. Even if it seems hopeless, keep praying.

4. *Make prayer an outpouring of your soul.* Fervent prayer comes from

the heart. It is more than words; it reflects the deepest desires of your soul. In fact, your words can even get in your way. The Bible tells us that God can hear and respond even to our "groaning" (Ex. 2:24). When you pour out your soul to God, you are connecting with Him at the deepest level possible. No pretense. No nice-sounding words. Just opening your heart to God as if your life depends on it.

Trust Explicitly

It's clear that even after Paul prayed fervently to be healed of his affliction, God didn't give him the answer he wanted. Instead, He basically told Paul to trust Him: "My grace is sufficient for you, for my power is made perfect in weakness" (2 Cor. 12:9). Not only was God telling Paul, "No, I am not going to heal you, even though you asked me three times to do it." He went a step farther and said, "Trust me. I know what I'm doing. I'm giving you my grace, and that is all you need."

Paul's response shows us what we should do when God's answer isn't the one we want to hear: "Therefore, I will boast all the more gladly about my weaknesses" (2 Cor. 12:9). You have probably heard preachers say that when you see the word *therefore*, you should pay attention to what it's "there for." In this case, it marks a transition; the apostle Paul was moving from his pleading to God to take away his problem to his willing acceptance of God's answer. In essence, he was saying to God, "Okay, this isn't exactly the answer I was hoping for, but You know what You're doing, and You always do what's best. I'm in."

It's one thing to trust God when everything's going right. But Paul shows us that even when our prayers don't receive the answer we want, we still need to trust God completely. This kind of trust led Horatio Spafford to pen the lines to the beloved hymn "It Is Well with My Soul." In 1873 this Chicago businessman put his wife and four daughters on a ship to Europe, where he planned to join them later for a family vacation. In the middle of the Atlantic Ocean, the ship was struck by another vessel and sank within twelve minutes. Spafford's wife was rescued, but their four daughters perished. As soon as he received the telegraph informing him that his daughters had drowned, he boarded a ship headed for Europe. When it reached the approximate spot where the girls had lost their lives, he stood quietly on the ship's bridge, then went below to his cabin and wrote, "Whatever my lot, thou has taught me to say, 'It is well, it is well with my soul.'"

Just seven years later the Spaffords lost their fourteen-year-old son to scarlet fever. Well-meaning members of the church they attended said the couple must have had some hidden sin in their lives for these tragedies to occur and asked them to leave the church, which they did. But the Spaffords' trust in God never wavered. Circumstances will occur that disappoint us, and people will say and do things that disappoint us, but God will never disappoint us. He is always with us, and He is more than enough for us.

When you trust God even when He seems distant, He begins to seem closer. Here are some ways to trust God explicitly.

1. *Show, don't tell.* Don't just tell God you trust Him and then keep worrying about the problem. Hand it over to Him completely.

2. *Believe that God really does know best.* The next time it rains, step outside and look at the rain fall. Millions and millions of raindrops will fall. God makes every single one of those raindrops. I love the way the psalmist describes God's control over the universe: "He determines the number of the stars and calls them each by name" (Ps. 147:4). If God is awesome enough to know every star by name, He is worthy of your trust. He is the same God that made you, me, every raindrop that falls, every star in the sky, and everything else, and He knows what is best for all of us.

3. *Avoid constantly asking the why questions.* Continually asking "Why me?" or "Why did God do this?" implies a lack of trust. In the Bible and throughout history, many of God's children have asked the one-word question "Why?" just as you and I have. It is not wrong to ask why, but it is wrong to remain camped out in the whys of life. If you believe God is sovereign and in control, then you know He is able to work good out of any and every situation. Romans 8:28 reminds us that "in *all things* God works for the good of those who love him, who have been called according to his purpose." That means that even when you don't get what you prayed for, you can still trust that God is more than capable of working it out for good.

4. *Focus on the present and future instead of the past.* You can spend the rest of your life looking backward, worrying about what happened and why it didn't happen the way you desired. God will allow you to do that. But if you do, you will miss the blessings of today and the blessings of the future that God has in store for you. Sometimes bad things happen, but live your life focused on today and on the future.

Prayer and trust go hand in hand. If you don't trust God, why pray? I will be the first to admit that when it appears that God is ignoring your prayers, it's difficult to trust Him. But I can also assure you that as you learn to trust Him no matter what, you will begin to see that He is worthy of that trust.

Evaluate Eternally

The final lesson we learn from Paul about how to deal with prayers that appear to be unanswered has to do with perspective. Three words from the passage in 2 Corinthians say it all: "for Christ's sake." Paul came to the place where he was able not just to tolerate his affliction but to actually "delight in weaknesses, in insults, in hardships, in persecutions, in difficulties" (2 Cor. 12:10) because they were part of God's eternal plan. In a sense, Paul was saying, "If that's what it takes for your kingdom to reign, it's fine with me." He knew that if God did not remove his affliction, it was for a higher purpose. He was able to view his "unanswered prayer" from an eternal perspective.

Paul also recognized that, in Christ's eternal perspective, his weakness could become a strength, but first he had to acknowledge his weakness. God will not release His strength into your life until you are willing to acknowledge your weakness. In the temporal world, this doesn't make sense, which is why so many Christians struggle in life and are discouraged. Too proud to acknowledge that they are weak, they instead try to make it on their own strength. If Paul had had a temporal focus, he would have been constantly depressed and defeated. When he wrote the letter to the Christians at Philippi, he was in a Roman prison! Yet Paul said, "Rejoice in the Lord always: and again I say, Rejoice!" (Phil. 4:4 KJV). How could a man who was put in prison for being obedient to God tell others to rejoice always? Because he could evaluate from an eternal perspective, not simply a temporal one.

When we evaluate life from a temporal perspective, we evaluate based on what we see with our eyes. When we learn to evaluate from an eternal perspective, we learn to evaluate based on what God shows us in our hearts. In John 17:3 Jesus provides a definition of eternal life. He says, " 'Now this is eternal life: that they may know you, the only true God, and Jesus Christ, whom you have sent.' " He said eternal life is having a relationship with God. God's Word says, "He has made everything beautiful in its time. He has also set eternity in the hearts of men" (Eccl. 3:11). God has given us a desire to look for something beyond today, and He has told us that eternal life with Him will be ours only if we have a relationship with Him and with His Son, Jesus Christ. Consider this wonderful encouragement from 2 Corinthians 4:16–18: "Therefore we do not lose heart. Though outwardly we are wasting away, yet inwardly we are being renewed day by day. For our light and momentary troubles are achieving for us an eternal glory that far outweighs

them all. So we fix our eyes not on what is seen, but on what is unseen. For
what is seen is temporary, but what is unseen is eternal." Having an eternal
perspective begins with having a personal relationship with God and focusing
on Him and His plans.

How do you evaluate life's circumstances from an eternal perspective as
opposed to a temporal perspective?

1. *Get in a helicopter.* Wouldn't it be great to have a friend in a helicopter
   above you when you're stuck on the interstate in a traffic jam? He
   could let you know how far it stretches and whether you should take
   the next exit or wait where you are, because he sees what's happening
   ahead of you. When God's answer to your prayer isn't the answer you
   wanted, try to look at it from His point of view rather than your own.
   He knows what lies ahead of you, and His answer is always based on
   that knowledge.

2. *Use the right scoreboard.* Since the world's idea of success is so different
   from God's idea of success, it is important that you use God's standard
   for keeping score. The world keeps score by looking at wealth, pos-
   sessions, recognition, and pleasure. God's scoreboard focuses on His
   plan to establish His kingdom. He is more interested in your character, your holiness, and your obedience to His Word. In His kingdom,
   everything is turned upside down, or maybe I should say right side
   up. For example, if you lose your job, you're a loser according to the
   world's scoreboard. You don't matter anymore. But according to God,
   your value and identity are wrapped up not in your job but in your
   relationship to Christ. You remain of invaluable worth to God. It may
   be that He has another position prepared for you that will allow you
   to have a greater impact for His kingdom.

3. *Look up, not around.* If you focus solely on your surroundings, you will
   soon lose sight of God and forget that He is in complete control of
   your life. You will measure yourself against your neighbors rather than
   by God's plan for your life. Tyler's family was able to cope better with
   his loss once they understood that God had a different plan for him
   than they did. They naturally wanted Tyler to be healed of his cancer,
   but God chose to use Tyler to inspire countless others through the
   hope he possessed in the face of death. God's plan was to demonstrate
   that His grace is enough to overcome the pain and grief of cancer,
   enough to defeat death, because Tyler lives on in heaven with Jesus. If
   it seems that God hasn't answered your prayer, look up, not around.

How to Trust God's Answer

Here's what to do when God's answer to your prayer isn't what you wanted or expected.

Recognize God's sovereignty. God is sovereign and allows things to happen for divine reasons that we may not understand in this life. If He does not give you what you asked for, be thankful for the role you are playing in His kingdom.

Remember how God has worked in the past. Focus on how God has cared for you in the past. Although it may not seem like it right now, He is still caring for you. If you put your complete trust in Him, whatever happens to you is part of His great plan to establish His kingdom.

Realize that this is not the end. Life here on earth is preparation for the eternity you will spend in heaven with God if you have accepted His Son as your Savior. Eternity is forever, making the seventy or eighty years we have on this earth seem like a heartbeat. If you didn't get the answer you wanted, it's because God knows the future and therefore knows what you really need.

Refrain from playing God. Make your wants and wishes known to God, then leave them in His hands. Don't tell Him what to do, and don't try to assume you know what's best for you. God's answer will be perfect because God cannot make a mistake. When you continually challenge His answer, you are in effect playing God.

Rededicate and surrender yourself to God. Take an honest look at yourself and evaluate where you are spiritually. Allow God to show you whether you have allowed sin or disobedience to creep into your life, and if you have, confess, repent, and recommit your life to God. Surrender means saying to God, "Not my will, but Yours."

God beside Us

Whether or not God answers your prayers in the way that you want, when you call out to Him, you can count on one thing: He is always there beside you, walking through whatever valley you face. This truth was recently illustrated in a letter I received from a friend of mine named Theresa. Theresa's father, a decorated Vietnam veteran, had been ill for some time, struggling with cancer. I joined Theresa and many others in praying for his healing, but he eventually died. About the same time, another friend of ours, Mike, experienced a rupture of an arteriovenous malformation (AVM) at the top of his spinal cord. This condition is usually fatal, but for reasons known only to God, Mike was healed, and he now actively shares his testimony of this wonderful miracle. Theresa wrote that while she was so glad for Mike and his family, she wished she had been the one able to stand before the church and share how God healed her father. Then she added, "But since my father's death, I've felt closer to God than ever before. He has comforted me and strengthened me in ways that I did not think possible, and though He didn't answer all of my prayers the way that I wanted them to be answered, He answered many of them far more generously than I ever could have imagined." The greatest blessing of all is that Theresa and her father will one day be reunited in heaven.

Not every prayer you pray will be answered by God exactly the way you want it answered. That's because God knows better than we do what we really need. He sees the bigger picture and knows exactly how you and I fit into it. He also knows that if we received everything we wanted, our lives would be a big mess! I thank God that sometimes He says to me, "No, André. I won't do that for you, but just watch Me work. I'll turn what you're going through into something good, far better than you can imagine. And through it all, I'll be right beside you."

What a great answer to prayer!

Creative
Conversations

When Dorothy, a pastor's wife and the mother of four children, was diagnosed with cancer, fear consumed her. "I could barely function, I was so scared," she explained. "The very word terrified me." What became especially frightening to her were the radiation treatments, because she had to lie flat on her back inside of a claustrophobia-inducing tube for what seemed like ages as the powerful rays zapped the cancerous cells in her body. "The only way I got through it was by reciting the Twenty-third Psalm."

Jim, a jogger in his late forties, was especially burdened about his teenage son who had begun experimenting with drugs, getting in trouble at school, and having some brushes with the police. It just tore Jim apart because it seemed as if there was nothing he or his wife could do to get through to Brian. One day while Jim was out jogging, the rhythm of his feet pounding the pavement coincided with words that formed in his heart: "Lord, bring Brian back." For the rest of his run, he mentally repeated these words over and over. "Those words just seemed to come to mind as I ran that day, and so from then on, every time I jogged, I repeated them."

Sherry, a young mother of two preschoolers, struggles with depression. Her husband's job requires him to travel a lot, and some days when he is gone, she can barely get out of bed to care for her little girls. She's careful to take her medication, which helps, but every now and then she is overcome with an impending sense of doom, and those are the days that worry both her and her husband. It was on one of those mornings that Sherry happened on a Christian radio station that was playing music that spoke to her heart. "The words of those songs I heard seemed to be the very words I wanted to say," she exclaimed. "I had never really listened to Christian radio before, but I became an instant fan, especially on those days when the darkness clouded my outlook."

What do Dorothy, Jim, and Sherry have in common? Even though none of them began with "Dear Lord," they were all praying. Dorothy let the words of Scripture that she had memorized become her prayer to God. Jim let his hobby of running become a "spiritual metronome" for his prayers. And Sherry let the lyrics of contemporary Christian music become her prayers.

Too many of us limit our idea of prayer by thinking that it has to be done a certain way. One of God's characteristics is that He is creative ("In the beginning God created . . ."). He invites us to share in His creativity in all areas of life, including prayer. While the purpose of prayer is always the same—communication with God—the methods can vary. Prayer may involve speaking—audibly or inaudibly—singing, listening, quoting Scripture, and writing. Each of these styles of prayer is a wonderful way to enjoy fellowship with God. The method or style of prayer we use is not nearly as important as praying to the one true God through His Son, Jesus Christ, and praying to Him without hindrance.

Talking to God

When you bow your head to give thanks before a meal, you're talking to God. When you kneel beside the bed of your four-year-old and say a nighttime prayer, you're talking to God. Most of what we consider to be prayer is simply talking to God. We rightly think of Him as a close friend or companion and just speak to Him. When you pray like this, you probably don't think too much about how incredible it is to be able to speak directly to deity, to the unchanging God who has overseen human history from the beginning of time. But this privilege goes back to the creation story, when God said, "Let us make man in our image, in our likeness, and let them rule over the fish of the sea and the birds of the air, over the livestock, over all the earth, and over all the creatures that move along the ground. So God created man in his own image, in the image of God he created him; male and female he created them" (Gen. 1:26–27).

This passage establishes our uniqueness before God. We are the only beings He created who bear His likeness and who are capable of having a relationship with Him. No other creature in all of creation was created in the image of God, which makes man special to God. And once He created man, it didn't take Him long to begin communicating, for in the very next verse of the creation account, God speaks clearly to a listening Adam and Eve, "Be fruitful and increase in number; fill the earth and subdue it. Rule over the fish of the sea and the birds of the air and over every living creature that moves on the ground" (Gen. 1:28).

As we learn in the sad account of man's fall from grace, the creation story makes it clear that God and man are able to communicate with each other. God places the first couple in the garden of Eden and tells them that they are free to do anything they want in the garden of Eden—everything but eat from a particular tree. When they disobey and eat from that very tree, we see the first recorded conversation between God and man.

When thinking of this story, most people place their attention on man's fall, and certainly that's an important element that establishes the doctrine of original sin—that man is inherently sinful because of the choice that Adam and Eve made. We often overlook another important element of the story: the reality of prayer. Man was given the wonderful privilege of being able to converse with God. This establishes a precedent which is repeated over and over again throughout the Bible: God and man relating to each other.

Although talking to God is the most common type of prayer, many people are intimidated by the idea of praying out loud. They see this type of prayer as what the preacher does during church, or maybe some super-Christian who knows all the right words to say. If you feel this way, you're missing out on a great relationship with God. What kind of relationship would you have with your friends if you never talked to them?

When you were a little kid, did you have an imaginary friend? Or if you are a parent, has your child ever had a make-believe person with whom they carried on conversations? This phenomenon is fairly common and gives us a picture of how to talk to God. He may be God, but He's also your friend. I love to listen to my youngest daughter as she engages in full-fledged conversations with her imaginary friends. They appear to be some of the best friends she has in the entire world, and she tells them everything in her plain and simple English. We can tell God everything too, only He isn't imaginary. We don't have to use religious language either. We don't have to kneel or even close our eyes. In the movie *Letters to God*, Tyler has such a close relationship with God that he will stop whatever he's doing and just talk to God or write Him a letter whenever he wants to. That's the kind of relationship God desires of us, that we never hesitate to talk to Him.

If you are not in the habit of talking to God, think of Him as a friend who is always at your side. Let's say you wake up with a headache but have a lot to do during the day: "Well, God, I'm not feeling too great. I need some help today." It's that easy. As you go through your day, share it with God by talking to Him. This is what the Bible means when it instructs us to "pray continually" (1 Thess. 5:17). Simply have an ongoing conversation with God in the same language you use when talking to your best friend.

Singing Your Prayers

If you visited a Jewish temple during a worship service, you would most likely hear a person singing in Hebrew. That person is a cantor, and his duty is to lead the congregation in prayer by singing the prayer out loud. In the historic liturgical churches, such as the Catholic and Anglican churches, prayers are often sung or chanted. Many of the praise and worship songs that are often used in Protestant and evangelical churches are really prayers set to music. That prayers are often sung to God shouldn't surprise us, because many of the psalms are songs that David wrote as prayers to God. He sang of his joys, his heartaches, and his desires. He sang praises to God as well as laments to God.

Have you ever considered singing your prayers to God? A friend of mine recalls how his mother used to sing hymns of the faith as she cleaned house: "She wasn't a professional singer by a long shot, and most of the time was off-key, but you could see by the look on her face that she was communicating with God as she dusted and folded the laundry." Now, David had a beautiful voice. It was so soothing that when King Saul became anxious or agitated, he often called for David to sing and play his harp for him. Maybe you, like David, have the kind of voice that people love to hear. Maybe not. It really doesn't matter. Most people love to sing, even if they can't carry a tune in a bucket. We sing in many places. We sing in the shower, and how many times have you looked over to the car next to you and caught the driver singing at the top of his lungs? People must think I'm crazy sometimes as they look over at me singing in my car. I'm just glad they can't hear me. Something about the act of singing allows us to express ourselves in ways that speaking does not.

One of the functions of prayer is to give thanks to God, to praise Him. The next time you feel grateful to God for something He has done for you, consider singing a familiar praise song. One of the more popular and traditional is the "Doxology":

> Praise God from whom all blessings flow.
> Praise him all creatures here below.
> Praise him above, ye heavenly host.
> Praise Father, Son, and Holy Ghost.

At your church, you may have learned contemporary praise choruses that serve as sung prayers. I enjoy singing "I Love You, Lord." It doesn't matter which song you sing as long as you sing it sincerely, from your heart to God. There is nothing magical about singing your prayers. Sung prayers don't work *better* than spoken or written prayers. But varying your approach to prayer will energize your prayer life, and singing out to God is one way to do that.

Praying the Scriptures

Have you ever started to pray but found you couldn't think of what to say? Or have you ever felt as if you're praying the same thing over and over and need a fresh way to talk to God? Consider praying the Scriptures. Some of the most beautiful and heartfelt prayers have been recorded in the Bible, many of them in the book of Psalms. Even though they were penned by someone else, they can become your own prayers. You might want to personalize them by inserting your name in appropriate places or by viewing them from your own needs and perspective.

Consider praying the following psalms for specific needs you might have.

Prayers of Praise
Psalm 30:1 – 2
Psalm 59:16 – 17
Psalm 66:20
Psalm 71:22 – 24
Psalm 145:1 – 3

Prayers of Confession
Psalm 40:11 – 12
Psalm 51:1 – 2
Psalm 79:9
Psalm 119:36 – 37
Psalm 130:1 – 4

Prayers for Help and Protection
Psalm 12:7
Psalm 31:1 – 5
Psalm 55:4 – 8
Psalm 60:5
Psalm 108:6
Psalm 141:3 – 4

Prayers of Trust
Psalm 5:11 – 12
Psalm 17:6 – 8
Psalm 18:35 – 36
Psalm 25:1 – 7
Psalm 77:11 – 14

Again, you can personalize these Scriptures by inserting your name. For example, the first line of the well-known Twenty-third Psalm would read like this: "The Lord is André's Shepherd, André shall not be in want." You can also pray the same prayer for your spouse or a friend or a son or daughter by inserting their names. While the naming of names may seem repetitious and awkward at first, it underscores God's desire to know you by name and to experience a close relationship with you.

Writing Your Prayers

As we learned in chapter 4, writing your prayers can add a whole new dimension to your prayer life. Written prayer is the most tangible type of prayer. In the more formal, liturgical churches, all prayers are written down and read aloud. People have sometimes been critical of written prayers for that reason, saying they are too formal, even impersonal. But when you instead think of them as letters to God, they are anything but impersonal.

Prayer as Listening

We've looked at the various ways we can talk to God: speaking, singing, quoting Scripture, and writing. All of these types of prayer involve our reaching out to God. But we've also learned that prayer is communication with God, a two-way street. So while prayer as listening isn't really a type of prayer, listening is a component of prayer that we can't ignore. In fact, regardless of the type of prayer we use, it's not really prayer if we don't also listen. But that's often easier said than done.

I remember as a kid hearing the older people from church say things like, "God told me to . . ." or, "Then God said to me . . ." It was as if they heard an audible voice from above actually speaking to them. Maybe they did. We know from the Bible that God has at times spoken so clearly and audibly that people actually heard Him. But I don't think it happens often, and while I have clearly "heard" from God, the only time I can recall ever hearing an audible voice was when I was a little boy, and I still have questions about that encounter.

So how do we listen to God if He doesn't talk out loud to us? Just because God doesn't always speak audibly doesn't mean He doesn't talk to us. I have heard God speak to my heart in a much louder way than any audible voice I have ever heard. In His sovereignty, God can impress His message on us in any way He wants. In his book *How to Listen to God*, popular television preacher and bestselling author Charles Stanley says that God generally speaks to us in four basic ways: though His Word, through other people, through His Holy Spirit, and through circumstances. Just as we can be creative in the ways we pray to God, He is even more creative in how He chooses to speak to us. But I have learned over the years that if we aren't listening, we will miss those times when God speaks to us. This is why we shouldn't be the only one doing the talking when we pray. It's easy to forget to listen to God, because we always seem to be in such a hurry. When we leave time to sit in complete silence and meditate on God, we have a better chance of hearing Him.

Often, before I read from the Bible, I ask God to speak directly to me about something I have prayed about or will pray about. Others conclude their prayers by saying, "Lord, speak to me through someone today." Many times when I have had to make an important decision, I have asked God to give me clear direction so that I can be certain of His will. Other times I simply remain silent, and God will bring a thought or an idea to my mind, which is often how the Holy Spirit works.

A beautiful passage in the Old Testament sheds some light on how God speaks to us: "The LORD said, 'Go out and stand on the mountain in the presence of the LORD, for the LORD is about to pass by.' Then a great and powerful wind tore the mountains apart and shattered the rocks before the LORD, but the LORD was not in the wind. After the wind there was an earthquake, but the LORD was not in the earthquake. After the earthquake came a fire, but the LORD was not in the fire. And after the fire came a gentle whisper. When Elijah heard it, he pulled his cloak over his face and went out and stood at the mouth of the cave. Then a voice said to him, 'What are you doing here, Elijah?'" (1 Kings 19:11 – 13).

Many of us are like Elijah, hoping to hear God speak to us in spectacular displays of power and might, when all along, He is quietly whispering to us. Thomas Merton wrote that "silence is the first language of God." I think what he meant is that to have a conversation with God, we must meet Him in silence. If you're in a crowded and noisy place and want to talk with someone, you probably would say something like, "Let's go outside, where it's quieter, so we can talk." That's what God is saying to us, inviting us to listen in silence so that we might hear Him. For some people, being able to listen to God requires turning off the television. For others, it requires turning off the DVD player, iPod, computer, cell phone, and any other device that distracts them so that they can sit in silence and listen for God's "still, small voice."

I'll admit that listening to God is not always easy. The second we end our prayers, we're ready to jump back into whatever we're doing. It's little wonder that we seldom hear God's voice. So whether you write your prayers as letters to God, sing your prayers to Him, speak your prayers out loud to Him, or read Scripture passages as your prayers to Him, as often as you can, follow your prayers with listening. Don't be in a hurry. Try to clear your mind of everything else and think of nothing but God. I try to listen to God twice as long as I talk to Him. God has given us one mouth and two ears, so we should consider using them proportionately. Most of the time, I sense from

God a direction I should go or feel led to do something specific. Even if you don't hear God's voice in the silence, continue to listen to Him throughout the day. Like Elijah, you may discover that God shows up in the most unexpected ways.

Part 2

Writing Your Letters to God

As we saw in chapter 7, prayer can take many forms, whether spoken, sung, or written. Many of the psalms exist as written songs and prayers to God, and throughout the Bible, many prayers are recorded in writing. Written prayers are no more effective than spoken prayers; what's important in praying is a sincere desire to communicate with God.

One benefit of written prayers is that reading them later can continue to inspire us as we recall what was going on in our lives when we wrote them. Written prayers can also inspire others, as the real Tyler's written prayers helped inspire his father to write the script for the movie *Letters to God*. Written prayers can have a huge impact on people, just as, in the movie, little Tyler's written prayers touched the lives of those who read them.

In the following chapters we will look at several different types of prayers, and then I will ask you to begin writing your own. You'll have plenty of space to practice, and when you are finished, this book will have an added and unique value to you: it will include a sampling of your own letters to God.

Once you have tried writing your prayers in letter form, I would encourage you to do two things. First, share them with a close friend or family member. If you are married, share them with your spouse. In this way, your letters will have a ministry of their own as they inspire others to develop a similar practice of writing their own prayers. And imagine in a few years having several journals filled with your written prayers. What a treasure to leave behind for your family and friends. Second, consider continuing this practice as a regular part of your quiet time with God. For me, writing my prayers to God has added a special dimension to my relationship with Him.

As you write your letters to God, keep these simple tips in mind.

73

1. Write letters, not formal essays or research papers. This isn't an assignment from your English teacher. Your letters should be just as informal and fun as notes to your best friend.
2. Write from your heart. Don't try to impress God with flowery language or perfect grammar. Record exactly what you're thinking.
3. Begin with a salutation or greeting, such as "Dear God," "Hello God," "Good morning, God." This may seem like a small thing, but it will keep your focus on God.
4. Be sure to indicate that you are coming to God through Jesus, by including something like, "In Jesus' name, amen."
5. Close with your name, just as you would close any letter. This personalizes the experience, closing the distance between you and God.

So grab a pencil or pen and get ready to begin an exciting journey of writing your own letters to God.

Praying for Yourself

Praying for yourself is often considered to be selfish. So much of what we're taught in the Bible and in church is to put others first. I recall being in a church and seeing a little poster with these words on it: "Jesus first, others second, yourself last." Jesus sacrificed His life for us, and He is our example of how we should reach out to others, how we should give of our resources rather than hoard them. It would make sense to follow that our prayers should focus outward as well, but interestingly, that's not the only way Jesus prayed, nor is it primarily how He taught us to pray.

If you recall from our brief study of the Lord's Prayer as a model for prayer, Jesus taught us first to honor God in our prayer ("Hallowed be thy name") and then to ask for sustenance for ourselves ("Give us this day our daily bread"). In fact, only one reference in this "perfect prayer" is made to others ("And forgive us our debts, as we forgive our debtors"; Matt. 6:9–12 KJV). But even this brief outward focus comes in the context of asking first for ourselves. Every other request in this prayer is for ourselves. I believe Jesus taught us to pray this way because God knows our needs and knows that if we do not ask for those needs to be met, we will be of little use to Him.

In an interesting passage in the gospel of John, we see Jesus spending a considerable amount of time explaining to His disciples that He will soon die and helping them understand how they will carry on without Him. It's almost as if He's giving them their final instructions concerning the church as we know it today, and He concludes with one of the most encouraging verses in the entire Bible: "In this world you will have trouble. But take heart! I have overcome the world" (John 16:33). The next time you feel like "the other side" is winning the battle, remember these words.

After going to great pains to explain what it will be like without Him and reminding His disciples that they are on the winning side, Jesus prays a lengthy prayer (John 17:1–26). The first person He prays for is Himself, basically saying, "I've done what You asked me to do, and it has brought You glory, so now please glorify Me with what I have to do next." Jesus knew that He would soon be arrested and nailed to a cross to die for our sins, and He prayed for Himself. As mentioned previously, in the other gospel accounts of Jesus' life and death, we see Him praying again for Himself just prior to His arrest, asking His Father to come up with some other way to redeem the world than through His becoming sin for us.

I remember leading a luncheon Bible study as part of a revival crusade years ago in Texas. The Bible study was on prayer. I was teaching the importance of praying for ourselves as part of our overall prayer lives. One lady was very proud that she had never prayed for herself. She thought it would be wrong to do so.

With all due respect for this sweet lady in Texas, there's nothing selfish about praying for yourself, especially if you understand prayer as a conversation and as one of the benefits of having a relationship with God. We think nothing of asking a friend for help from time to time, and God invites us to do the same with Him. We are His children, and as the perfect Father, He loves to care for our needs: "How great is the love the Father has lavished on us, that we should be called the children of God!" (1 John 3:1).

Several times in the New Testament we are given the promise that we can ask God for anything and He will give it to us. That bothers some people because they have prayed for something for themselves and God didn't give it to them. They conclude either that these verses aren't trustworthy or that we shouldn't really ask God for anything. Both responses are wrong. Everything in the Bible is true, but to understand a particular verse correctly, we have to consider the whole counsel of Scripture. In the case of this promise, we must consider all of what God's Word teaches, and when we do, we learn that two conditions must be met if we expect God to give us what we ask for. First, we must always make our requests in the name of Jesus (John 16:23–24), and second, we must always ask according to God's will (1 John 5:14). We also need to understand that God cannot do anything contrary to His character and that He won't give us anything that could harm us. So when you pray for yourself, ask Him to meet whatever you honestly need or desire and then trust Him to do what's best for you. His way is always the best.

What, then, should you pray for when you pray for yourself? Begin by praying for the three things mentioned in the Lord's Prayer: daily sustenance, forgiveness, and deliverance from sin or anything that would displease God. If God specifically tells you to pray for these things, it must be important to Him. In our culture of plenty, we probably don't pray that often for "our daily bread," but some interpret this prayer to include both our physical nourishment as well as our spiritual nourishment. So for those of us who have plenty, often too much, to eat, maybe we should be praying for God to give us more of an appetite and desire for Him. When we think of it that way, the model Jesus provided in the Lord's Prayer suggests that we ought to pray daily for our spiritual health — for a closer relationship with God, for forgiveness of anything we have done to displease Him, and for protection from the temptations that come our way. Not a bad way to begin our prayers for ourselves.

One of the great examples of a man praying for himself again comes from David, after being confronted by the prophet Nathan for committing adultery with Bathsheba. Not only had David had an illicit relationship with her, but he had sent her husband, Uriah, to the front lines of a fierce battle and instructed his field general, Joab, to withdraw the troops so that Uriah would be killed. Nathan calls David out for what he did, and Psalm 51 records David's agonizing prayer for himself. He begs for mercy. He pleads for God to show him compassion. He asks to be cleansed of this awful sin, to be washed "whiter than snow" (Ps. 51:7). Finally, he asks God to restore the joy of his salvation and give him the resolve never to let this happen again.

I recently heard about a man who was a prominent pastor and author who similarly fell into an inappropriate relationship with a woman. It was devastating to his wife and his family, and it forced him to leave the ministry. This incident happened more than thirty years ago, and by God's grace, he has since restored his relationship with his wife. While he no longer pastors a church, he works for a Christian organization and is a walking testimony to God's grace and forgiveness. God has used him to counsel young pastors about the need to live holy lives, and he urges them to pray every day for strength to avoid temptation. "This is the first thing I pray for myself when I wake up every morning," he says.

Several years ago, while attending a conference, I heard D. James Kennedy tell a fellow pastor that he would not allow a computer in his house or office unless it had an internet filter. Dr. Kennedy was stressing the importance — even, as he described it, at his "older age" — of protecting yourself from the temptations that can come from the internet.

I love the simple and straightforward way the book of James invites us to take our "business" to God: "Is any one of you in trouble? He should pray" (James 5:13). So many of our prayers are tame and therefore unrelated to what's really going on in our lives. I think that's partly because we try to hide from God when we pray. We feel a little like Adam and Eve when they suddenly realized they were naked and were ashamed before God. Trust me, God knows what you're going through and is right there in the trenches with you, whether you realize it or not. Instead of "Dear God, please make me a better person," God wants to hear prayers that reveal what is really going on in your life: "Dear God, please help me avoid internet pornography today."

When you write letters to God asking for your own needs and desires, be specific. The wise man of God I mentioned earlier who once committed a grievous sin now prays every day for protection from sexual temptation, not just from temptation. Here's a list of things to consider writing to God about.

- *Your role as a spouse or as a parent.* Do you have any special needs in these areas? For example, do you have a problem with anger or a lack of patience? Have you grown distant from your spouse? What specifically do you want God to do for you in these roles?
- *Your job.* Are you "on the bubble," possibly facing the loss of a job because your company was recently sold or is not doing well? Do you have a difficult assignment that is creating stress for you? Do you have a boss or colleague you can't stand? Why try to handle these things alone, when God wants to help you with them?
- *Your finances.* This is closely related to praying for your "daily bread" or sustenance. I have heard countless stories of people who found themselves in dire financial difficulty and asked God to provide for them, and God came through in unexpected ways. We have to be careful here, because when it comes to money, we can be motivated by greed. God expects us to be good and generous stewards of our money. If you're in huge debt because you spent foolishly on things you don't need, God may answer your prayer simply by allowing you to live with the consequences of your selfishness so you will mature through the experience.
- *Physical challenges.* Have you ever asked God to help you lose weight? Why not? Have you ever prayed for more energy? God wants you to enjoy the body He designed for you. Be careful here, though. He may answer you by nudging you to do a better job of taking care of yourself. I know of athletes who always pray before a game, but never to win, only that they play up to their potential and that God protects them. When it comes to the World Series or the Super Bowl or any other sporting event, God cares more about the people participating than about who wins.

- *Bad habits or addictions.* Have you tried without success to quit smoking? Are you dependent on alcohol or any other drug to have a good time or to relax? Tell God about it in your letter. Be honest with Him and ask Him to take control of any destructive habits that you have. Let this prayer become a good habit to replace the bad one. Don't limit your prayers to only the "safe" areas. God loves it when we level with Him.

- *Major (and minor) decisions.* I simply cannot imagine making a major decision without first taking it to God and listening for His guidance. Perhaps the most important decisions you can make as a parent are the ones that affect your children. Should she transfer to a private school? Should I homeschool them? Should I let him buy a car? When should I let them start dating? With our kids, hardly any decision is minor. Do you pray about those decisions?

- *Big dreams or ambitions.* Have you ever thought you'd like to quit your job and start your own business? Or do you secretly wish you could go on a mission trip with your church, but you don't think you could raise the money or your spouse opposes the idea? There's an old chorus that says, "God specializes in things called impossible." The Bible is filled with seemingly impossible situations made possible when people cried out to God.

- *Peace of mind.* Do you worry a lot? Do you have difficulty falling asleep because you're thinking of all the things you have to do tomorrow? In His Sermon on the Mount, Jesus exhorts us not to worry. That's easier said than done, of course, but I find that when I take my worries to God, He gives me a sense of peace and well-being. I may still have a lot of stress in my life, but talking to God about it eases its effect on me.

Your Best Self

While it may intially seem selfish to devote so much time to praying for yourself, as you practice this type of prayer, you will learn why it is so important. If you've ever flown on a commercial flight, you have heard the safety instructions from the flight attendant regarding the oxygen mask: "If you are flying with children, put your own oxygen mask on before assisting your children with theirs." Why? Because if you don't take care of yourself, you can't be of much help to anyone else. God wants each of us to know Him and to have a close relationship with Him. He knows that when we are strong and are walking daily with Him in faith, we will be better able to serve Him. I have known too many pastors who have poured themselves into their ministry to the extent that their own spiritual lives suffered, and they eventually left the ministry. I love my congregation, and I love my wife even more, but if I am to serve them as I should, I need to pray for myself as much as I pray for them.

Before you begin writing your prayers, I'd like to share two prayers that you might want to pray or to adapt as your own. The first comes from the Book of Common Prayer, which is a collection of prayers, Scripture readings, and special services used in the Anglican Church.

> This is another day, O Lord. I know not what it will bring forth, but make
>   me ready, Lord, for whatever it may be.
> If I am to stand up, help me to stand bravely.
> If I am to sit still, help me to sit quietly.
> If I am to lie low, help me to do it patiently.
> And if I am to do nothing, help me to do it gallantly.
> Make these words more than words, and give me the Spirit of Jesus. Amen.

The second prayer is from German pastor Reinhold Niebuhr and is often called the Serenity Prayer.

> God, grant me the serenity
> to accept the things I cannot change,
> courage to change the things I can,
> and wisdom to know the difference,
> living one day at a time,
> accepting hardships as a pathway to peace,
> taking, as Jesus did, this sinful world as it is,
> not as I would have it,
> trusting that You will make all things right,
> if I surrender to Your will,
> so that I may be reasonably happy in this life
> and supremely happy with You forever in the next.

Now spend some time reflecting on your own life and your needs and desires. What challenges do you face that seem insurmountable? What do you want God to do for you, in you, through you, and with you? Over the next few days, use the space provided to write letters to God, asking Him to help you in any area of your life. To help you begin writing you prayers, I am sharing one of my own.

> Dear God,
>   Sometimes I am almost overwhelmed with what it means to be a

dad. My kids are great, but I know they live in a world so different from the one I grew up in. Please calm my fears for them. Help me trust that You will take care of them. Please help me know how to answer their questions and give me the courage to say "I don't know yet" until I do. I especially need You to show me the right way to help guide them in their choices without making all of their decisions for them. Help me have the courage to say no when I need to, trusting that they eventually will understand why I did. I guess I'm just asking You to help me be a better dad. Thank you for listening. I'm asking all these things in the name of Your Son, Jesus. Amen.

———————— **Personal Prayer** ————————

—————————— **Personal Prayer** ——————————

———————— **Personal Prayer** ————————

Praying for Your Family

If you are a parent, you don't need me to tell you that caring for a family is a huge, almost daunting responsibility for which we never seem to be fully prepared. My wife and I have read many wonderful books on parenting, and we've benefited from the godly teaching of more experienced parents. Every parent should similarly seek out expert advice on parenting, because it's the most important job you will ever have. But even with all the help we've received, it seems like every day we face something that wasn't covered in the books or seminars. We've also learned that each child is different. When you have six children, that makes for a lot of differences. What worked for one might prove disastrous for another, but who knew?

Although I do not have scientific proof of this, it seems that the evil forces working against our families are stronger and more serious than ever. I'm not an alarmist by nature, but consider some of the realities facing our children today.

- One-third of America's ninth graders have engaged in sexual activity. By the twelfth grade, that number jumps to two-thirds.[2]
- According to the US Justice Department, in 2008 more than three thousand arrests were made for internet crimes against children.
- Parents are being recommended to have their daughters vaccinated for the sexually transmitted disease HPV when they are eleven years old.[3]
- People aged twelve to twenty drink 11 percent of all the alcohol consumed in the United States.[4]

- In a survey of high school students, 45 percent reported that they had drunk alcohol within the past thirty days, 18 percent reported that they engaged in "binge drinking," 11 percent had driven after drinking, and 29 percent had ridden with someone who was driving after drinking alcohol.[5]
- The typical preschooler who daily watches about two hours of cartoons will be exposed to ten thousand violent incidents per year. Five hundred of those preschoolers are at high risk of modeling aggressive attitudes and behaviors.[6]
- In combined scores of mathematics and science literacy, twelfth graders in the United States ranked eighteenth out of twenty-one countries on the 1995 Third International Mathematics and Science Study (TIMSS) assessment.[7]
- The average cost of college for one year is $11,300 for public universities and $27,600 for private colleges.[8]

I'm not saying it has ever been easy to be a parent, but the more I read the newspaper and listen to what's going on in our culture, the more time I spend on my knees praying for my family. My children are growing up in a world in which things that were once considered out of bounds even for movies are now regular fare during "family viewing hours" on network television: profanity, partial nudity, sexual promiscuity. We take for granted program names such as *Sex in the City, Desperate Housewives,* and *Californication.* Values that we try to teach in the home are often ridiculed, if not outright challenged, by popular television programs. And that's just television. The types of things that can happen with our kids on the internet almost make my head spin, and if you don't know what "sexting" is, you'd better learn, especially if your child has a cell phone.

Are you ready to start praying for your family?

The Bible makes it clear that as parents we have a responsibility for teaching our children how to live for God. After giving His people the Ten Commandments, God told them, "Impress them on your children. Talk about them when you sit at home and when you walk along the road, when you lie down and when you get up" (Deut. 6:7). In other words, teaching your children moral principles should be a full-time job. Because our kids spend so much time away from us and under the influence of others, sometimes it feels as if we're trying to guide our children with one hand tied behind our backs. We are in a battle for our families. Fortunately, we have a special weapon if we would just use it: prayer. As far as I'm concerned, the two most important things we can do for our children are to model godly lives for them and to pray for them.

In 1984 a somewhat ordinary mom named Fern Nichols was about to send two of her children off to middle school. She felt almost physically overcome by a huge burden for them, knowing that they would be exposed to vulgar language, bullying, peer pressure, and ideas from teachers and students that conflicted with what was taught in their home. It weighed on her so heavily that she cried out to God for their protection and asked Him to send her one other mom who felt the same way she did and who would be willing to meet with her and pray for their children. God sent her that woman. And another. And many more, enough to launch a movement known as Moms in Touch. Moms in Touch offers a simple yet powerful resource that is being used around the world: one or more moms gathering to pray for their children and their schools, including the teachers and administrators. It operates now in more than 120 countries. In the United States alone, 17,500 schools are being prayed for throughout every state.[9] This great organization began with a mother's burden. I believe that God gave that burden to Fern and that He wants each of us to feel the same overwhelming desire to pray for our families.

I know of a man in his fifties who learned that his elderly parents kept a list of all their children, grandchildren, and great-grandchildren — a total of forty-two names — on three index cards kept in his father's Bible. "My father told me that ever since my oldest brother, their first child, was born, they started each day by praying for him, and as their family grew, they added the names to their list," he recounted. "What's amazing to me is that over these three generations of relatives, there hasn't been a single tragic accident or serious injury. Three family members were diagnosed with cancer and all are in remission, some for twenty years. None of my siblings or their extended families have experienced major financial problems or loss of work, and to the best of my knowledge, all of them love the Lord and attend church regularly. I have to believe my parents' daily prayers for us have something to do with the good fortune that our family has experienced." Although prayer does not guarantee us that everything will always work out perfectly for us, we are guaranteed the privilege of prayer, and we should faithfully practice it on behalf of our families.

What Your Children Need

The most important prayer you can pray for your children is for their salvation. As I look back on the events of his short life, I am so privileged to have helped lead little Tyler Doughtie into a saving knowledge of Jesus Christ, but I know that his parents also regularly prayed that he would one day come to know Jesus personally. We never know what will happen tomorrow with our children, but we know that if they have given their hearts to Jesus, they will live with Him forever in heaven. If you have a son or daughter who has not decided to follow Jesus, pray that the Holy Spirit will gently nudge them to recognize their need for the Savior.

Stop reading. Put this book down and spend some time right now in prayer for your children. Pray for each one by name and ask that they will one day come to know Jesus as their personal Lord and Savior. Mark this page and come back to it regularly as you pray for the salvation of each of your children and grandchildren.

List the names of your children and grandchildren below.

Pray also for your children's protection. Obviously, we want them to be physically safe, but also pray for their spiritual and emotional protection. Unfortunately, kids can be pretty cruel to each other. Bullying has become a major concern in schools and other places, but even seemingly innocent name-calling and teasing can hurt a child enough that it affects his or her ability to do well in school. As parents, we wish we could go with our children everywhere and protect them from all the dangers they face. That's not possible, of course, but we can pray for them, asking God to place a barrier of protection around them.

As your children get older — middle school age and above — pray for them to be strong in resisting peer pressure. Your kids most likely know the difference between right and wrong and genuinely want to do what's right. But they also want to fit in. As parents, we often think it's easy to "just say no," but was it easy for you when *you* were thirteen? Take a closer look at the temptations your kids have to face each day. Maybe instead of only telling our kids to say no, we should tell them, "Today I'm going to be asking God to give you the courage to do what's right whenever one of your friends tries to get you to do something wrong." And then follow up by praying throughout the day for God to do exactly that.

Many churches conduct an infant dedication ceremony; parents bring their babies to the front of the church as a symbolic act of dedicating them to God. We call ours a parent-child dedication service. These dedications are based on several events in the Bible, including one when people brought their children to Jesus so that He could pray for them. Jesus' disciples thought this was beneath Jesus and tried to turn the people away, but Jesus said, "Let the little children come to me, and do not hinder them, for the kingdom of heaven belongs to such as these" (Matt. 19:14). In many of these dedication services, parents are asked if they will promise to pray for their children and nurture them in their faith. If you made such a promise when your children were babies, how well have you kept it? And if you have never made a promise before God to pray regularly for your children, why not do it now?

That Other Member of Your Family

I have found that most parents understand the need to pray for their children, even if they don't always consistently follow through on that need. If I ask them if they pray for their spouses, however, I sometimes get a blank stare. Given the pressures on our marriages, doesn't it make sense to pray for our spouses? A wise pastor once counseled a couple who poured themselves into their children's lives, "You're focusing way too much on your kids. If you don't pay more attention to each other, what's going to happen when your kids leave home?" The same could be said about praying for our kids. We need to do it, but not at the expense of praying for our spouses.

If you aren't in the practice of praying for your spouse, try this sometime: before you go your separate ways in the morning, say something like, "I'd like to pray for you today. What would you like me to pray about for you?" You may need to be prepared for a brief fainting spell. But seriously, I truly believe that praying for our spouses helps strengthen our marriages. There is something quite touching and profound about knowing that my wife will be praying for me throughout the day, and vice versa. If we've had a disagreement or were a little grouchy with each other, it's hard to keep that spirit going when you bow your head to pray for each other. We need to take a moment with our spouse to voice a prayer together and then be faithful in praying for the issue or concern regularly throughout the day.

You know the specific needs of your spouse, but if you need some starter ideas, consider these: encouragement, safety, good health, good friends, success at work, godliness, contentment. I also pray that my wife's love for me will remain strong. That may sound odd, but I have seen too many marriages of church people grow cold, so I want God to be at work in that area as well.

I have six wonderful children and a terrific wife, so that might explain why praying for my family consumes a major portion of my prayer time. I can't play favorites, so I am including a sample prayer for each of them. I believe it's important to pray for our family members by name and to pray specifically for their unique needs. Read the sample prayers to help you get started, then use the space provided to write your own prayers for your family:

> *Dear God,*
>
> *Thank you for blessing me with my wife, Sarah. Please bless her in a special way today as she walks with You. Guide her as she teaches our children today. Please help her listen carefully to You and obediently follow You in all You lead her to do. Thank you for gifting her in teaching and writing, and I pray You will continue to use her through both.*
>
> *In Jesus' name, amen*

> *Heavenly Father,*
>
> *Please bless Jed as he is away at college today. I pray that he will look to You and follow You in every decision he makes. Help him study hard and do the best he can do on all of his tests and projects. May he live in such a way that he honors You at all times. Please allow him to excel in music and drama, as You have gifted him in these areas.*
>
> *In Jesus' name, amen*

> *Dear Heavenly Father,*
>
> *I pray that You will bless Joshua in a wonderful way today. I ask that as he works today, You will allow him to be a great witness for You through both his work ethic and his words and deeds. Please give him clarity concerning Your desire for his future. He seems to enjoy helping people through various technological means, and it appears You have equipped him to do so. Please use him in this way to glorify Yourself.*
>
> *In Jesus' name, amen*

Dear Lord,

I lift Caylee to You today and ask You to help her as she studies. She has such a desire to write songs and books and to honor You through acting. Please continue using her in these ways for Your glory. I also pray that You will use her as she demonstrates Your love to the children for whom she cares. May her love for You and her love for life continue to shine through her.

In Jesus' name, amen

Dear God,

I lift Joseph to You today and ask You to work in his life in a powerful way. You know far better than I do the stresses and temptations that a teenager like him faces. Please help him understand the need to walk close by Your side. Lord, he has a desire to be used through athletics, and it appears You have gifted him in this area, and I pray that if this indeed pleases You, You will allow him to excel in athletics and to use his ability to honor You.

In Jesus' name, amen

Dear Heavenly Father,

Please watch over James in a special way today. He has such a love for You and for other people. You have placed within him a desire to invent and be creative, and I pray You will allow him to continue to use the creativity You have placed within him to honor You. He loves to talk—he's a lot like his dad that way—please guard his words so that they reflect You at all times. I also pray he will always have the deep desire he now has to lead others to You.

In Jesus' name, amen

Dear Lord,

I lift my little Caitlyn to You and ask that You will keep Your hand of protection on her. Thank you for her love of singing; please help her always sing as if nobody else is around. You have made her so sensitive to the needs of others; please allow her to continue to demonstrate love to those around her. I pray that she will always realize that she is Your little girl as well as my little girl and that she will remain close by Your side.

In Jesus' name, amen

Personal Prayer

—————————— **Personal Prayer** ——————————

—————————— **Personal Prayer** ——————————

Praying for Someone Who Is Seriously Ill

Because I'm a pastor, people often turn to me in their distress. A child has run away from home. A husband and father has lost his job. A family member is arrested. Fire levels someone's home. These are all heart-wrenching situations, but few things create as much grief and confusion as having a friend or loved one become gravely ill, either through disease or an accident. We have come to dread words like *Alzheimer's, leukemia, quadriplegic,* and *coma* because they usually mean we can expect a long and difficult journey of suffering with little hope for our loved one's recovery. When our children had their bouts with strep and the flu, we prayed for them with clear expectations that they would get better. When a friend is diagnosed with a terminal illness, our prayers often become questions.

Even as I write this, a friend of mine is dying of cancer. As far as the medical community is concerned, his type of cancer is incurable. My friend is a committed Christian who believes God has the power to do anything. He knows that when he dies, he will enjoy an eternal reward of perfect health in heaven, but he desires to live longer here with his family instead of having his life cut short by twenty years or so. So he has boldly asked God to heal him. So have I, along with perhaps hundreds, if not thousands, of people who know about his illness. Although God has allowed him to live longer than most men live who have his type of cancer, the cancer still exists. As far as we know, God has not healed him.

I know of another man whose mother was diagnosed with an aggressive form of ovarian cancer forty years ago. Prior to her surgery to try to remove the tumor, she knelt in her living room, and her husband and sons knelt beside her, placed their hands on her shoulders, and prayed a simple prayer asking God to heal her. She had the surgery, then one round of chemotherapy. After one year, her cancer was in remission. After five years, she was declared cancer free. Her oncologist said he had never seen anything like it in his entire career.

Two stories of people who prayed earnestly for their sick loved ones. Two different outcomes. Did God answer one prayer and ignore the other? Did God heal the woman with ovarian cancer or did the chemotherapy destroy the cancerous cells? Do our prayers even matter?

These kinds of questions have perplexed people for ages. And we have come up with all sorts of answers to try to explain how God works. Some people say that if you pray for healing and it doesn't happen, it means you don't have enough faith or that there's unconfessed sin in your life. At the other extreme are people who claim that God performed miraculous healings only during a certain period in time but, in our modern times, has chosen to suspend His healing power. In my opinion, there are some things our finite minds simply cannot fathom or explain, and I believe both of these extreme views underestimate God's ability to do what He wants to do.

When it comes to praying for people who are sick, here are four things that I do know with great certainty. First, God is sovereign and all-powerful. He is in complete control of the universe and has the power to do *anything*, and whatever He does is good and just. His will is perfect, meaning that His control over everything has a divine purpose: the establishment of His kingdom. We, on the other hand, have limited knowledge and therefore cannot always understand why things happen the way they do. What this means for us on a practical level is that if we pray for a friend to be healed and that friend continues to be sick, we can still trust God. The movie *Letters to God* beautifully illustrates this through the life *and* death of little Tyler. His family, friends, and church all prayed for him to be healed, but God used Tyler's illness to draw others closer to Him. Sometimes we see God's purpose immediately, sometimes that purpose becomes clear to us much later, and sometimes we may never learn why God chose to do what He did or why He allowed certain things to happen, until we meet Him in heaven. It is not our job to understand; our job is to trust God.

Second, God always answers our prayers, but He doesn't always give us what we ask for. If you pray for a loved one who has an incurable disease and ask God to heal her, God might answer yes, He might answer no, and He might answer "not yet." But whatever He answers, you can trust that He knows exactly what He is doing and will use His answer to bring about a higher good. Remember, the apostle Paul prayed to God three times to heal him of an unspecified condition that tormented him, and God's answer was always the same: No. Perhaps Paul's affliction was necessary so that he would learn and then teach all of us the glorious truth that, regardless of the burdens we carry, God's grace is sufficient to help us triumph over our weaknesses.

The third thing I know for sure about praying for the sick is that God expects us to do it. Throughout Jesus' ministry, people brought their sick friends and loved ones to Him. Because Jesus cared about the physical well-being of people and healed the blind and the lame, we call Him the Great Physician. It is only natural, then, that we call out to Him on behalf of those who are sick; we are carrying out a ministry that has characterized Christians since Jesus walked the earth. In our church, when we learn that someone is seriously ill, our people mobilize, and hundreds of prayers go out on that person's behalf. One of the greatest ministries in our church is our prayernet ministry, a prayer ministry through email, which allows hundreds of people to be informed in a matter of seconds of a need for prayer or a cause for praise. This is simply our modern-day version of the telephone prayer chains that some churches use to spread the word that prayers are needed for someone who is sick. What's so wonderful about these prayer chains is that often they spread to other churches, and people across the country and around the world join in to pray for someone they don't even know!

This brings me to one last thing I know with certainty about praying for the sick: it is a privilege that benefits both the person praying and the recipient of the prayers. Prayer brings people together and reminds us what it means to be a part of the body of Christ. It often shows us how big and loving and compassionate God's family is. When I pray specifically for someone who is seriously ill, I am pulled into that person's life in a way that probably would not have happened otherwise. That person might be hundreds of miles away in a hospital bed, yet I am right there beside him, lifting his needs to God. When we pray for someone who is suffering, we experience a spiritual intimacy that changes us forever. And if you are on the receiving end of those prayers, it is almost overwhelming to realize that your brothers and sisters in Christ are calling out to God on your behalf.

Several years ago, I experienced a very serious illness. I developed a severe case of diverticulitis, which resulted in a perforated colon, surgery to remove one foot of my colon, and the infiltration of E. coli throughout my body. I spent ten days in the hospital and three months recovering as my wife nursed me back to health. While this was a difficult experience, it was also a very blessed one. I personally know of over two thousand people who faithfully prayed for me during this time, and I was told of thousands more, both in this country and around the world, who lifted me to the throne of God.

It is hard to put into words the phenomenal encouragement I received from knowing that so many people were praying for me. Some of the people who prayed for me took the time to come and pray with me in person. An incredible bond developed between us as they poured out their hearts to God on my behalf. It has been my privilege to pray for countless people throughout my life, and it has been my joy to have countless numbers of my brothers and sisters in Christ intercede for me. The blessings of prayer are indeed wonderful.

God Heals in Many Ways

It is quite normal that we want God to heal our friends and loved ones who have been struck with an incurable disease or a serious illness. We should never hesitate to ask God to heal them, but we should be prepared to let God heal in His own way and in His timing. I have known people who were never physically healed of a disease but experienced an "inner healing" that transformed their understanding of God in such a way that enabled them to cope with their illness far better than anyone could imagine. In fact, my friend who has cancer has become something of a star patient of his hospital's cancer center because God has given him such a great attitude about his illness. The hospital staff loves to see him come in for his treatments because he brightens the place with his smile and kind words to everyone. Some people have even come to faith because of him.

I have also known of cases in which a serious illness brought healing to broken families. A few years ago, a man in his seventies who had served the Lord all his adult life fell ill, and the doctors informed the family that his condition was terminal. His family gathered at his bedside and prayed for a miracle, that is, all but one of his sons, who had abandoned his faith some thirty years prior and had cut off all contact with his family. Somehow, however, he learned about his father's illness and returned home, to the surprise of the entire family. God chose not to heal the father but performed an even greater miracle, the healing of severed family ties. Stories like this remind us that when we pray for those who are seriously ill, we should give the situation to God and trust Him to care for it. Someone once said that the perfect prayer is, "Thy will be done," meaning that whatever God chooses to do is exactly the right thing.

A Heavenly Perspective

When we ask God to heal someone who is seriously ill, we're basically asking Him to let that person live longer. That's understandable, because no one wants to lose a loved one, yet one comfort we have as Christians is that our time on earth is only a brief preparation for what is in store for us in the future. God has already performed the greatest miracle of all through the death and resurrection of Jesus. "Where, O death, is your sting?" (1 Cor. 15:55). Jesus defeated death, giving those who believe in Him eternal life in heaven. When a loved one who is a believer dies, the natural sadness we experience is tempered by the knowledge that we will one day be reunited. I'm still sad that my natural parents died when I was young, but I'm looking forward to seeing them again and spending eternity with them.

God's promise of eternal life is why we do not look at death as His failure to answer our prayers. To those who have no hope—those who reject Jesus—death is a tragic sentence to eternal separation from God, but to those who believe, it is a homecoming. The funerals of Christians are not somber services but celebrations. Yes, we are sad to lose a relative or friend, but we know that instead of saying goodbye, we're really saying, "See you later!"

So when you pray for someone who is suffering from a serious illness, pray boldly for healing. Also ask God to comfort not only the person who is sick but his or her friends and family members as well. Pray that God will use everything about the illness to draw others closer to Him. I also try to remember to pray for the caregivers—doctors, nurses, and others—because He uses them to comfort and even heal the sick.

Many times serious illnesses, especially those involving young children, test our faith and cause us to ask questions, so use your prayer to talk to God about any questions you have. Some well-meaning Christians believe it is wrong to question God, but when Jesus was hanging on the cross, He cried out to God, "Why have you forsaken me?" (Matt. 27:46). If Jesus, who was without sin, can question God, so can we. Remember, prayer is a conversation with God, and conversations often involve questions. He always welcomes your questions, and if you listen patiently, He will answer them.

It is my sincere hope that no one in your family is seriously ill. But there's a good chance you don't have to look far to find someone who needs your prayers, perhaps someone in your church or at work or maybe a parent of one of your kids' friends. Once you have someone in mind, read through my sample prayer and then write your own prayers for this person. In addition, I would like to challenge you to put some feet to your prayers. Visit the person you have been praying for if it is possible, and consider reading one or more of your prayers to him or her. Again, I cannot adequately express the blessings I received from having people come to pray with me during times of need. Your taking the time to share your prayers with someone who is sick may be just what they need to get through the day.

> *Dear God,*
>
> *Please allow Fred to know You are with him today in a special way. I know that he has been going through some intense pain. Why, God? He's been so faithful to You. Sometimes I just don't get it, but I do trust You, Lord. I know that You have already used Fred to inspire others, and that You have a bigger purpose in all of this. Just the same, could You give him some relief today? Could You just wrap Your arms around him and let him know You love him? And Father, will You somehow let him know that I and many others love him too? I'm asking for this in Your Son's name, Jesus. Thank you, Lord.*

———————————— **Personal Prayer** ————————————

Personal Prayer

————————— **Personal Prayer** —————————

Praying for Your Leaders

We Americans love to talk politics. Sooner or later, our conversations come around to whatever the political hot issue of the day is. The economy. Health care. Education. The economy. Term limits. The economy. Taxes. More troops. Fewer troops. Did I say the economy?

During an election year, the talk seems to get longer and louder. And "election year" is a misnomer. It's more like election *years*, for the campaigns seem to start the day after the previous election. Like most people, I get a little tired of it sometimes, but I have my opinions and am willing to share them with anyone who wants to know how I feel. One of the privileges of living in a free and democratic society is that we can openly discuss any concern we have. Every Memorial Day, I'm reminded again that men and women fought and died to give me the freedom to vote for our leaders and to express any concerns I have, both with those I voted for as well as with those I didn't. I'm also reminded that whoever gets elected faces a tough job that directly affects my welfare and the welfare of my family as well as that of every other person in our nation and often others around the world.

Have you ever considered praying for your leaders?

Praying for the President

In an interesting part of the apostle Paul's letter to Timothy, Paul not only exhorts us to pray for our leaders but explains why: "I urge, then, first of all, that requests, prayers, intercession and thanksgiving be made for everyone—for kings and all those in authority, that we may live peaceful and quiet lives in all godliness and holiness" (1 Tim. 2:1–2). This was written at a time when Christians were being harassed by "those in authority," yet Paul said to pray for them, even to be thankful for them!

When was the last time you said a prayer of thanksgiving for your president or governor?

If I asked you to describe your world for me, you probably wouldn't use words like "peaceful and quiet" or "all godliness and holiness." Could that be because we spend more time complaining about our leaders than we do praying for them? What might happen if every Christian committed to pray every day for our national and community leaders? What if we prayed for them to have wisdom to pass laws that reflect the morality expressed in the Ten Commandments? What if we prayed for their salvation as fervently as we pray for the salvation of a son or daughter?

Great writer on prayer E. M. Bounds once wrote, "God shapes the world by prayer. The more praying there is in the world, the better the world will be, and the mightier will be the forces against evil." So often we pray for peace or justice or a return to godly values, but we never pray for the people who could help bring about those things. Shortly after President Barak Obama was elected, Richard Land, president of the Ethics and Religious Liberty Commission of the Southern Baptist Convention, wrote an open letter to him promising to pray for him, his family, and his administration. He said that he would ask God to bless him with safety, health, and spiritual blessings. And he recommended that all Christians do the same. As he wrote on his website, "It is likely that, as with every person who has occupied the White House in our lifetimes, we will disagree with at least some of President Obama's positions on social and moral matters. If we contend with his decisions with bitterness and an unflattering spirit, we run the risk of bringing dishonor on the name of Christ."[10] In other words, it doesn't matter if the president is a Republican, a Democrat, independent, or of any other political persuasion; it is our responsibility as Christians to pray for him.

Shortly after the terrorist attacks on America on September 11, 2001, a group of Christians formed an interesting internet resource called the Presidential Prayer Team (*www.presidentialprayerteam.com*) to help people pray intelligently for President Bush and other leaders. Now that we have a new president, this helpful website calls on Christians to pray for him as well. I try to be careful about recommending websites because I know that many can be misleading or promote agendas that do not align with Christian teaching. But this one appears to be fair and nonpartisan and describes its purpose as "to encourage Americans to unite in fervent prayer for their country." It explains the various issues facing the president and suggests prayers for each particular issue. It even lists the president's daily schedule so you know who he is meeting with and can pray for those meetings.

One well-known event concerning prayer for our leaders and our nation is the National Day of Prayer. The National Day of Prayer Task Force website (*www.ndptf.org*) provides this information about the National Day of Prayer:

> The National Day of Prayer is an annual observance held on the first Thursday of May, inviting people of all faiths to pray for the nation. It was created in 1952 by a joint resolution of the United States Congress, and signed into law by President Harry S. Truman. Our Task Force is a privately funded organization whose purpose is to encourage participation on the National Day of Prayer. It exists to communicate with every individual the need for personal repentance and prayer, to create appropriate materials, and to mobilize the Christian community to intercede for America's leaders and its families. The Task Force represents a Judeo-Christian expression of the national observance, based on our understanding that this country was birthed in prayer and in reverence for the God of the Bible.

This group also provides weekly prayer tips and sponsors prayer summits, among other things. The greatest thing you and I can do is pray. If you want to see our nation become the nation God desires it to be, you must commit to regularly praying for our leaders. I am so thankful for this group and others like it that help keep us focused on the importance of prayer.

The president of the United States is often called the most powerful man in the world. Whether or not that's true, he is the commander in chief of our military, he has the power to veto legislation, and he commands the respect of world leaders. As citizens of our nation, it is our right to disagree with him, criticize him, and vote against him if we want to. But as citizens of the kingdom of God, it is our privilege and responsibility to pray for him.

Praying for Local Leaders

Some of the leaders who have the greatest immediate influence over our lives are various community leaders: mayors, city managers, police chiefs, fire chiefs, school superintendents and board members, and other leaders. The decisions they make often affect us directly and determine the type of community we live in. These leaders are almost daily under tremendous pressure from various special-interest groups and community factions that have agendas that sometimes conflict with Christian values (gambling, adult entertainment, legalization of marijuana, etc.). I know of a church in the Midwest that used to invite their town's mayor to church at the beginning of every year just to pray for him. A group I mentioned previously, Moms in Touch, also prays for school leaders, believing it is as important to pray for principals and superintendents as it is to pray for their own children.

A word of caution, however. When praying for our national or local leaders, it is tempting, especially if we say our prayers publicly, to use prayer as a bully pulpit or to make a point. I've heard well-meaning pastors lead *prayers* that are more a tirade to criticize an elected official than they are prayers. I don't think that's what Paul had in mind when he urged us to pray for those in authority. Here are the kinds of things we should ask for when we pray for our leaders.

- *Safety.* Sadly, our leaders are often targets. The more visible and powerful the leader, the greater the danger. Presidents are followed constantly by the Secret Service for this reason, and other leaders are not immune to threats. Even local politics sometimes results in an angry person threatening to harm or kill the leader with whom they disagree.
- *Wisdom.* Imagine having someone with you at all times who is carrying what is known as "the football," a briefcase containing the code that is needed to launch a nuclear attack. That knowledge alone should lead us to pray for our president, but all leaders have to make tough decisions that demand great wisdom. As I write this, many states and municipalities are having to make huge budget cuts. How would you like to decide between cutting meals for senior citizens and free school lunches for children in need?
- *Courage.* Pray for leaders to have enough courage to stand by their convictions. Many elected officials go into their jobs with clear convictions and high ethical standards and then discover the pressure that comes from lobbyists and other special-interest groups. It takes great courage to vote against a law that you feel is wrong when one of your biggest donors wants you to vote in favor of it.
- *Spiritual guidance.* Pray that our leaders, even if they are not followers of Christ, will look to God and the Bible for guidance. Most of the good laws that form the foundation of our nation were written by men who, though they may not have all been Christians, believed in God and trusted the Bible, and we should pray that our leaders recognize that. The Bible is filled with wisdom that, if followed, leads to a prosperous and productive life for individuals and, collectively, for a nation.

"It's lonely at the top" is a phrase we sometimes use to describe a condition of leadership. As a leader of our church, I know I have sometimes been misunderstood, and I have had to make decisions that were unpopular with some of the dear people in our congregation. One of the great privileges of leading a church, however, is knowing that the people you lead are praying for you. It is a great comfort to know, before I step into the pulpit to preach, that someone prayed for me and the message I will be delivering. Walking into a meeting when I know we will have to make difficult decisions is just a little easier because I know that people are praying for me even as I start the meeting. Their prayers help take the loneliness out of leadership, but more important, I believe their prayers make me a better, more effective leader.

One leader in your life whom I hope you always remember to pray for is your pastor. Your pastor is under constant attack from all sides. Satan would love to destroy pastors who are growing God's kingdom. Pray for the physical, mental, emotional, and relational protection of your pastor. Pray for your pastor's marriage and family. Pray specifically for his purity in his relationship with his wife. Pray for God to use him and speak through him as he preaches, and prepares to preach, each week. Be a praying encourager for your pastor. *Encourage* literally means "to put courage into." Pray for your pastor and his family frequently. Write your prayers for your pastor as letters to God. As you feel led, share your prayers with your pastor as an encouragement to him. By praying for your pastor, you can be used of God to "put courage into" him and strengthen him for the calling God has placed on his life. Faithfully pray for your pastor and other ministers at your church each week, if not daily.

I know that you won't be able to pray every day for each and every leader who has an impact on you and your community, but I would like to suggest that you join me and millions of other Christians in praying regularly for our president. Then select at least one other group of local or national leaders to pray for on a rotating basis as well, for example, your school president and board members, your governor and other state leaders, your mayor and other city or town leaders and your pastor and other ministers. Read through the sample prayer below and then write your own prayers for your pastor and leaders in the space provided.

Dear God,

Thank you for allowing me the blessing of living in a country where I can vote for the person I feel led to vote for and that I can express my favor or my discontent with decisions that are made. I understand that I am blessed with the opportunity to pray for those who serve in leadership positions. I lift to You today our president. I pray that You will give him a desire to know and do Your will. I pray that You will protect him and his family. I ask You to please help him have a clear understanding of the sanctity of life and that this understanding will be evident in the decisions he makes. May he receive and follow Your wisdom in making decisions that affect those who live in our country as well as those who live around the world.

In Jesus' name I pray, amen

───────── Personal Prayer ─────────

Personal Prayer

————————— **Personal Prayer** —————————

Praying for Your Enemies

I love the Bible. I really do. I love reading it, studying it, teaching it, and preaching it. But wouldn't life seem a lot easier if a few verses just sort of disappeared from the Bible? Not better, but easier. For example, that verse about turning the other cheek when someone hits you. I *know* it's the right thing to do, but come on, do I have to? Then there's the teaching about being slow to speak and quick to listen. I'm a preacher!

But perhaps the most difficult teaching from the Bible is slipped into the middle of the Sermon on the Mount: "Love your enemies and pray for those who persecute you" (Matt. 5:44). Unfortunately, we can't delete or ignore verses in the Bible that we don't like or that seem impossible to obey. Jesus was preaching to His followers, people who came from great distances to hear Him teach about the way they should live as Christians. He knew that anyone who associated with Him would be persecuted, perhaps even killed, so this teaching takes on even greater meaning. Later, He demonstrated this very teaching by asking His Heavenly Father to forgive those who nailed Him to the cross. Jesus knew the powerful witness that comes from demonstrating love to those who are opposed to us. One of the reasons the early church prospered was the way that believers responded to their enemies, and we are asked to do the same thing.

Who Are Your Enemies?

Who exactly was He talking about when He told us to love our enemies? Some scholars suggest that Jesus was referring to governments or institutions. That would mean that if you were a Christian in America during World

War II, your enemies would have been the Japanese and German governments because we were at war with them. It might also mean that today we are called to love the people behind the terrorist attacks on our nation. That's a pretty tall order. Others say Jesus was referring to individuals in our lives whom we really dislike because they have treated us or our loved ones poorly. So if you have a colleague at work who is spreading false rumors about you or deliberately trying to make you look bad, you are to love her. That's not very easy either.

I think Jesus was referring to both. We are called to love and pray for anyone who could be considered an enemy, whether it's an enemy nation or an individual who hates us. To put it more bluntly, Jesus is telling us to love and pray for our enemies whether they be Osama bin Laden or your next-door neighbor. Nations, armies, and other political institutions, after all, are made up of individuals, human beings created and loved by God. It is this kind of love for the enemy that led an American soldier named Jacob De Shazer, who was tortured in a Japanese prison during World War II, to return after the war as a missionary to the very people who tortured him. De Shazer was one of the Dolittle Raiders who dropped the atomic bomb on Nagasaki, Japan, and later was captured by the Japanese. In the final days of the war, while he was still in a Japanese prison, he felt God calling him to love his captors: "I felt love toward the Japanese people and a deep interest in their welfare. I felt that we were all made by the same God and that we must share our hardships and our happiness together. How I wished that I could tell the Japanese people about Jesus! I knew that my Savior would be their Savior too."[11]

DeShazer loved his enemies and he took it to the next level by praying for them. After all, we are instructed not only to love our enemies but to pray for them too. It's certainly hard enough to love someone who has done something bad to you, but you can say you love someone and still maintain a certain emotional or physical distance. Praying for them means you actually have to be concerned about them. You have to *do* something. There's nothing indifferent about prayer. When you pray for others, you have become an ally, a partner, in their lives. You pray for God to reach out to them. You pray for their salvation. You pray for their forgiveness. Jesus doesn't let us off easy here. He knew that our prayers would be the evidence of our love. Regardless of how severely we are wronged, our job is not to punish or strike back but to pray for those who wronged us.

Why Bother?

By now, you have a long list of people to pray for: your children, your spouse, people who are sick, the president, other leaders, and your pastor. Do you really need to add enemies to your list? In this teaching, Jesus implied that praying for our enemies is related to our eternal reward in heaven: "pray for those who persecute you, that you may be sons of your Father in heaven" (Matt. 5:44–45). Jesus understood that the common response to enemies fosters bitterness and hatred, and He offered a radical way to protect us from those ungodly qualities. Our enemies usually bring the worst out in us. When you carry a grudge against someone who mistreated you, the initial hurt becomes magnified, and ultimately the desire to get even can destroy you. But when you find it in your heart to see that person as Christ sees her and you lift her up to the throne of God in prayer, you free yourself of all the anger and pain she caused you, and in the process, you demonstrate the love of Christ to someone who needs it.

Praying for our enemies is a spiritual discipline that helps us become more Christlike. We sometimes refer to Jesus as "the Lamb that was slain," because He did not retaliate or fight back as He was led to the cross. The Bible tells us that He could have easily called ten thousand angels to come and rescue Him, but He instead chose not to resist and chose to forgive His enemies. Something about this image has drawn people to Him ever since, and when we respond to our enemies with love instead of revenge, it disarms them and opens their hearts to God. I truly believe that we are in a time of intense spiritual warfare and that our Christian values are being threatened. We can see our enemies clearly, and seeing them invading our culture sometimes makes us angry. While I believe we should fight evil wherever we see it, praying for the enemies we fight against protects us from hating them. So many times we say we "hate the sin but love the sinner," but our actions betray those noble intentions. You can't pray for someone and hate him at the same time.

Finally, we pray for our enemies out of obedience. Jesus makes it quite clear that this isn't optional: "I tell you" (Matt. 5:44). Just as God hasn't given us the Ten Suggestions, Jesus' difficult teachings in the Sermon on the Mount aren't optional. These ethical teachings help distinguish us as followers of Christ, as opposed to followers of false religions. Yes, it may appear that it would be a lot easier if we were not required to love and pray for our enemies, but God has called us to a higher standard because so much is at stake: our own spiritual well-being and the potential salvation of our enemies.

It may be that the individual you consider to be your biggest enemy didn't do anything to you directly but hurt one of your children or another family member or friend in a big way. Sometimes it is more painful when someone we love is hurt than when we ourselves are hurt. God the Father certainly knows what it means to have someone He loves be severely hurt. I can't even imagine what God experienced as He watched His one and only Son be nailed to the cross and treated like the worst criminal who ever lived. And remember, those who are responsible for Christ's death are not just the people in the crowd gathered at the mock trials and surrounding the cross at Calvary; you and I are equally responsible.

In spite of all we did to His Son, God loved us. That is beyond amazing to me. Jesus willingly gave Himself for us and chooses to forgive us, and His Father is willing to allow us to come into His family. If God can forgive us and love us, and if Jesus can continually intercede for us, certainly we can learn to love, forgive, and pray for those who are our enemies or the enemies of our loved ones.

Here are some tips to help you prepare to write your prayers for your enemies.

1. *Identify who your enemies are.* Who has treated you or your loved ones so unfairly that you can barely bring yourself to even think about them? Who evokes strong feelings of dislike in you?
2. *Identify what they have done to become your enemies.* Why do you consider them your enemies? What have they done?
3. *Reflect on your enemies as little children.* At some point, every enemy was once a little child in the arms of its mother, and thinking of that will help move us toward forgiving our enemies.
4. *Imagine what you would say to God about your enemies.* What do you want God to do with them, or for them?

You may need to reflect on these questions for a few days before you are ready to pray for your enemies. And you may first have to pray for God to help you forgive them. Only then will you be able to write prayers for your enemies. I hope my sample helps you.

Dear God,

You know everything, so I know You understand how upset I am because of what Bob did to my wife. I honestly want to go over to him and knock his head off, but I also know that doing that at this time would not result in anything positive. He says he is one of your children, but he doesn't act like it at all. Either he doesn't really know You or he is completely out of fellowship with You. Either way, he needs to be in a close, loving relationship with You. God, I ask You to help Bob realize that what he did is wrong, and I pray that he will come to You for forgiveness and that he will acknowledge that what he did to Sarah was wrong. Please help Sarah and me forgive Bob and love him the way You love him and the way You love us.

In Jesus' name I pray, amen

———————— **Personal Prayer** ————————

—————————— **Personal Prayer** ——————————

Personal Prayer

Praying through Sorrow

Have you ever gone to church with a heavy heart? Perhaps you got some bad news during the week—an aging parent was diagnosed with Alzheimer's, a nephew was sent off to Afghanistan, a friend's husband left her. As everyone else around you was singing a praise chorus, did you feel as if they must be living charmed lives? Most likely you were singing too, but your heart wasn't in it. You didn't want anyone to think you weren't spiritual, so you went through the motions of praise and worship, yet deep inside, you were crying out in anguish.

Let me share a little secret: you weren't the only one in that congregation carrying a burden so heavy you could barely move. From where I sit in church, it would be easy to think that the happiest people in the world go to our church—people smiling, greeting each other, singing, wearing fine clothes. Many of them are just like you; they are crying inside but hold back their tears in church because they don't want anyone to think something's wrong. I have to admit I've done the same thing myself.

Life is filled with sadness. You don't have to be a pastor or a genius to know that even the most outwardly happy person may be just barely hanging on. We've been taught, especially men, to keep a stiff upper lip. In church, a long face or sad countenance is often interpreted as a sign that we've lost our joy for the Lord, so a lot of us wear happy-face masks when we go to church. Let's clear something up right now: it's okay to be sad. Being a follower of Christ does not guarantee terminal happiness. The only guarantee our faith gives us when it comes to sorrow is that we never have to go through the dark valleys of life alone.

As I mentioned in chapter 2, by the time I was sixteen years old, I had experienced a great loss: my birth parents died within four years of each other. Like anyone who loses a loved one, I went through all the stages of grief. But the one that lingered the longest—and still appears from time to time—was sadness, the aching emptiness of heartbreak that makes you cry until you run out of tears and then you cry some more. Sometimes I wondered if I would ever be able to smile or laugh again, and if I think too much about it even now, I can feel a lump forming in my throat. I was fortunate to be surrounded by the love and care of many godly people who gently tried to help me get through the darkness of my sorrow. I often wonder how people who are not part of a caring Christian community get through sad times, because these dear saints were so helpful to me. The new family God provided for me, including my new parents, Jack and Lou, was instrumental in helping me through this time. But as I reflect on that time in my life, I realize that the greatest resource for a grieving person is prayer. My Christian family, friends, and mentors were great, and I am thankful for them, but they couldn't always be by my side. Many times I would be all alone: alone in the darkness of my bedroom; alone in a crowd of students; alone as I walked to a friend's house. But I wasn't alone, and I used those times when no one was around to really have it out with God. He took all my questions, absorbed all my anger, and every time I finished talking (even yelling), He gently answered, "I'm still here. I understand. I know how you feel. I lost My Son, you know. We're going to get through this."

Sometimes I think God allows sorrow in our lives because He knows that's when we will seek Him desperately and honestly. It gives Him the greatest opportunity to show us He is all that we need. Some of my most treasured times with God have come when I have been at my lowest.

Have you ever seen the silent cry of a toddler? A little girl looks around and can't find her mommy, she opens her mouth to cry, and no sound comes out as those big raindrop tears form in her eyes and slowly begin to slide down her chubby little cheeks. If you've ever seen this, what was your natural reaction? You wanted to go pick her up and hold her close and reassure her that her mommy would be right back. That's the image I have when I think of how God responds to our sorrow: our Father in heaven reaching down to hold us in His arms when we are sad.

The Bible gives us many examples of people crying out to God in their sadness. In fact, one entire book of the Old Testament is called Lamentations, which basically means "mourning" or "grieving." The writer is mourning the destruction of Jerusalem, including the destruction of the temple, and the followers of God being driven out to live in exile. Listen to some of his laments and try to recall your own thoughts when you have cried out to God in anguish. Can you relate to any of these cries from Lamentations?

Is any suffering like my suffering?

—Lamentations 1:12

This is why I weep and my eyes overflow with tears. No one is near me to comfort me, no one to restore my spirit.

—Lamentations 1:16

See, O LORD, how distressed I am! I am in torment within, and in my heart I am disturbed.

—Lamentations 1:20

My eyes fail from weeping, I am in torment within, my heart is poured out on the ground.

—Lamentations 2:11

Do not close your ears to my cry for relief.

—Lamentations 3:56

Joy is gone from our hearts; our dancing has turned to mourning.

—Lamentations 5:15

Why do you always forget us? Why do you forsake us so long?

—Lamentations 5:20

One of the most hauntingly beautiful descriptions of a mother's cry and God's loving answer is found in the book of Jeremiah. While it specifically refers to God's promise to rescue Israel from captivity, it can be especially meaningful to any mother or father of a child who has run away or turned his back on the faith he has been taught. "This is what the LORD says: 'A voice is heard in Ramah, mourning and great weeping, Rachel weeping for her children and refusing to be comforted, because her children are no more.' This is what the LORD says: 'Restrain your voice from weeping and your eyes from tears, for your work will be rewarded,' declares the LORD. 'They will return from the land of the enemy. So there is hope for your future,' declares the LORD. 'Your children will return to their own land'" (Jer. 31:15–17).

One of the things I love about the interplay between David and God in the psalms is that despite his sorrow or frustration with God, David always comes to a point of trust in his prayers. For example, in Psalm 13 he asks, "How long must I wrestle with my thoughts and every day have sorrow in my heart?" and then later says, "But I trust in your unfailing love; my heart rejoices in your salvation. I will sing to the LORD, for he has been good to me" (Ps. 13:2, 5–6). This prayer and other similar prayers are great models for how to pray when we are grieving. It's okay to unload on God, to question Him, to express your frustrations. I sure did when my mom died. But if we stay in that mode very long, we rob ourselves of the relief that comes when we reflect on God and what He has done for us: He has saved us, given us another day to serve Him, and promised to walk with us through the valley, and He will use the trial we are going through to bring about something better.

Dark Days

I would venture to say that when it comes to the death of a loved one, most people instinctively turn to prayer to help them cope with their grief. Even people who do not claim to have faith in God are likely to say a prayer to "someone out there." Dealing with death is often a wake-up call and turns our hearts heavenward. But grief and sorrow come not only from the loss of a loved one. As finite humans living in a fallen world, we will experience many events that darken our days with sadness: the loss of a job, a divorce, a friend's betrayal, financial troubles. I know some people who no longer watch the news because it fills them with sadness to see images of suffering caused by earthquakes, floods, and other natural disasters. Even things that should make us happy can make us sad. Have you ever witnessed a high school graduation? They say the tears in a mother's eyes are tears of joy, but they are also shed because Mom knows her nest soon will be a little emptier.

If prayer helps us get through the major tragedies of life, shouldn't we turn to God in prayer when we experience these normal and more frequent times of sadness, even if they are momentary? When we do, we not only experience God's presence and help in our time of trouble, but the help that we receive equips and motivates us to reach out to others. The apostle Paul describes God as "the Father of compassion and the God of all comfort, who comforts us in all our troubles, so that we can comfort those in any trouble with the comfort we ourselves have received from God" (2 Cor. 1:3–4). Something contagious happens when we take our sorrows to God in prayer. It's like having a migraine and discovering a treatment that wipes out the excruciating pain. It turns you into an evangelist for that treatment. You can't stop telling your friends about it, especially any friends who suffer from migraines. When God meets you in your sorrow and lifts you from your sadness, you want to tell everyone, "It works! You don't have to carry your burdens alone. Ask God to lift your spirits when you are sad, and He will do it."

Praying in Steps

Psychologist Elizabeth Kubler-Ross identified five stages of grief that we go through when we lose a loved one: denial, anger, bargaining, depression, and acceptance. As you write letters to God when you are sad or grieving, focus on the anger, depression (sadness), and acceptance of your situation. Often, when something makes us sad, we respond with anger at God for allowing it to happen. I believe it's healthy to express that anger to God in our prayers, and I've already cited from the Bible several examples of David practically shouting at God. God already knows about your anger. He wants you to communicate with Him openly and honestly. Expressing your anger is part of that communication when you are going through a difficult situation. Some of your prayers may simply be an expression of your sadness and depression, laying them out there for God, letting Him *know* your heartbreak. Finally, as you continue praying to God about your sorrow, He will lead you into acceptance. When you reach this point, you will be able to acknowledge that even if you don't understand why something happened, you accept it. You will recognize that God is sovereign and that the loss that you have suffered will be used for His glory.

Read through my sample prayer and then write your own prayers about burdens you are carrying that make you sad.

Dear God,

I know that You are well aware of everything that is happening. Part of me is hesitant to say this, but I know that You want me to be honest with You. I am so angry about what Terry is doing. He is hurting my family and he doesn't seem to care at all. What really makes me mad is that You are not stopping him, and I know You could. Why won't You? It doesn't seem fair to me. Even though I am mad, I am trying to trust You. I am choosing to trust You, but it is hard for me. Please help me. Thank you. I love You.

In Jesus' name, amen

———————— **Personal Prayer** ————————

———————— **Personal Prayer** ————————

—————————— **Personal Prayer** ——————————

Praying as Worship

What comes to mind when you hear the word *worship*?
Most of us think of worship as something we do together in a church building. And it is, but it is so much more than that. Regardless of the type of church you attend, there is likely a time of singing, preaching, and focusing on praising God. Many churches, including my own, have a senior pastor and an additional full-time staff member whose responsibility is to lead the congregation in various experiences of worship. Few things are as stirring as hearing the people in our church raising their voices in prayer or song to God.

But you don't have to be part of a large group to worship God. *Worship* literally means "worth-ship," or the giving of worth to something. For Christians, worship means giving God all the honor, glory, and praise that He deserves, and you don't have to wait until you're at a church service to do it. In fact, sometimes you can't avoid worshiping God on your own. Have you ever stepped out onto your deck or pulled back the shades of your windows just as the sun was rising, and you were overcome with gratitude to God for giving you such a great day to be alive? That feeling of thankfulness and joy welling up inside of you is the unquenchable desire to worship God — to give Him credit, to acknowledge that He's the one who created such beauty and chose to give you such a spectacular glimpse of it that morning. And what better way to do that than in prayer?

The book of Psalms provides us with many models of written prayers as worship. Perhaps the most well-known, and in my opinion the most beautiful, is Psalm 8, which begins, "O LORD, our Lord, how majestic is your name in all the earth!" Consider just a few other worship prayers from the book of Psalms:

The heavens declare the glory of God; the skies proclaim the work of his hands.

—Psalm 19:1

Many, O LORD my God, are the wonders you have done. The things you have planned for us no one can recount to you; were I to speak and tell of them, they would be too many to declare.

—Psalm 40:5

I will praise you, O LORD, among the nations; I will sing of you among the peoples. For great is your love, reaching to the heavens; your faithfulness reaches to the skies.

—Psalm 57:9–10

How lovely is your dwelling place, O LORD Almighty! My soul yearns, even faints, for the courts of the LORD; my heart and my flesh cry out for the living God.

—Psalm 84:1–2

For you make me glad by your deeds, O LORD; I sing for joy at the works of your hands.

—Psalm 92:4

I will exalt you, my God the King; I will praise your name for ever and ever. Every day I will praise you and extol your name for ever and ever.

—Psalm 145:1–2

Throughout this book of songs and poems, it seems as if the writer, often David, experiences epiphanies and just can't contain himself. Even in the middle of a complaint, he will stop and honor God with praise and worship. In Psalm 41, David complains about enemies who slander him, and even a close friend who betrayed him, but ends his rant with these words: "Praise be to the LORD, the God of Israel, from everlasting to everlasting" (Ps. 41:13). One of the great things about having a relationship with God is that we can unburden our hearts to Him anytime we want. Sooner or later, however, we find ourselves drawn back to the desire to worship Him. It's almost as if once we bare our hearts to Him, expressing all of our fears and frustrations, we recognize again just how fortunate we are to be able to talk to almighty God, and that's when what we think of as worship usually begins.

If you've ever been in love, you know what worship is all about. We sometimes jokingly use the phrase, "He worships the very ground she walks on," but it's not far from the truth. While true worship should be reserved for God, when you are in love, you find it natural—even irresistible—to lavish your lover with words of praise and adoration. Often we do that by writing letters. You may not think of him as a romantic type, but Winston Churchill often wrote love letters to his wife, always beginning, "My darling Clemmie." And I'm guessing that if I found a box of letters you wrote to your spouse in the earliest days of your relationship, I would discover similar terms of endearment. After all our years of marriage, I still get a thrill out of writing a love letter to Sarah. Love makes us do things like that.

Similarly, our love for God often creates the desire to let Him know how we feel about Him. We were created with a natural passion for our Creator. We were made for the purpose of passionately knowing and loving God, and prayer is one of the ways we express that to Him. Worshiping God through prayer not only pleases God but reminds us of what He has done for us. Too often we get bogged down with our problems and turn to God only when we need help solving them. Imagine being on the receiving end of that conversation. Certainly, God invites us to bring our cares and burdens to Him, but how would you feel if all that your children did was ask for things? Think of how it feels when, out of the blue, one of your kids says, "Thanks, Mom. I'm so glad I have you for a mom!" Through Jesus, we are given the awesome privilege of having a relationship with God, and as our Heavenly Father, hearing us worship Him with praise and thanksgiving must surely please Him.

The challenge, of course, is to make our worship consistent, to remember first to worship God in our prayers rather than allowing it to be hit-or-miss. I have found that I am more likely to worship God in my prayers when I take the time to reflect on His greatness and how He has blessed me. Even if I'm having a bad day or going through a difficult time, when I pause to focus my thoughts on God, it puts me in an attitude of worship. Most of us can report certain basic blessings in our lives.

- We are alive to experience another day.
- We have family and friends to share life's journey.
- We have a roof over our heads, clean water at the turn of a faucet, and adequate clothing—things that at least one billion people in the world do not have.
- We have plenty, maybe too much, to eat.
- We have received an education at least adequate enough to allow us to read these words.
- We live in a land where we can worship freely, a nation blessed with

more churches of every size, style, and denomination than any other nation on earth.

Those are just the basics. To prepare for worshiping God through your prayers, in the space provided, list as many things as you can think of for which you are thankful. To get you started, I have listed a few blessings from my own life.

- A wonderful, loving, faithful wife who knows and loves God
- Children who have each given their hearts to Jesus
- The privilege to serve God as a pastor of a great church
- I was recently in a car accident and survived!
-
-
-
-
-
-
-
-
-
-

Now go back over the list and read each entry out loud, adding these words after each one: "Way to go, God! Thank you" (or any other expression of praise and worship). If you're in a secluded place where no one will think you're crazy, shout your expression of worship. I recently learned of a young man who has a big heart for God and is not hesitant to express his love for Him. He is an adventurer and has done a lot of hiking on the Appalachian Trail, and he says that every now and then while he's hiking in the wilderness, he will be so overcome with a sense of God's presence in the mountains and the forest that he will shout at the top of his lungs, "Hallelooooooooooooia!" You don't have to do that, but worship does have an emotional, even physical, quality. The final psalm exhorts us to praise God with trumpets, cymbals, and even dancing.

Write Your Worship to God

Can you dance in a letter? I'm not sure, although it might be fun trying, but either way that shouldn't keep us from writing letters to God that worship Him. To help you get started, remember that worship is simply giving God all the honor, glory, and praise He deserves. It is acknowledging that all the good in our lives comes from Him. A worship letter to God could simply be a sentence or two thanking Him for a specific blessing you experienced that day. I try to keep track of answers to prayer and then use my worship time to thank God for those answers, even for the answers I didn't want. Use the following blank pages to record your letters of worship to God. Focus specifically on how God has worked in your life, how He has met your needs and provided for you at home and at work. In a way, these are your personal psalms of praise, and you will find it inspiring to go back and read them from time to time. As a sample, I have included one of my own letters of worship to God.

Dear God,

I worship You and You only as the one true God. You alone are worthy of my worship. This week was very difficult for me, but through it all, You were there. I could feel Your presence. How awesome to have You beside me. How comforting to know You care. What a privilege it is to know You. Thank you for helping me get through this week. Thank you specifically for helping me resolve that disagreement I had with my friend. You gave me just the right words. That was all You, God. Wow! I praise Your name. You alone are worthy of my worship.

In Jesus' name, amen

—————————— **Personal Prayer** ——————————

—————————— **Personal Prayer** ——————————

———————— Personal Prayer ————————

Appendix

Applying What You've Learned

This appendix contains information for couples and prayer partners, small-group leaders, pastors, and church leaders interested in incorporating into their various areas of ministry the practice of writing prayers.

Using Written Prayers with a Partner

God wants us to pray alone, and He also wants us to pray with partners. His Word teaches about the power of praying together and illustrates the importance of willingly and regularly participating in prayer with others.

Acts 12:1–19 demonstrates the power of praying with partners:

> It was about this time that King Herod arrested some who belonged to the church, intending to persecute them. He had James, the brother of John, put to death with the sword. When he saw that this pleased the Jews, he proceeded to seize Peter also. This happened during the Feast of Unleavened Bread. After arresting him, he put him in prison, handing him over to be guarded by four squads of four soldiers each. Herod intended to bring him out for public trial after the Passover.
>
> So Peter was kept in prison, but the church was earnestly praying to God for him.
>
> The night before Herod was to bring him to trial, Peter was sleeping between two soldiers, bound with two chains, and sentries stood guard at the entrance. Suddenly an angel of the Lord appeared

and a light shone in the cell. He struck Peter on the side and woke him up. "Quick, get up!" he said, and the chains fell off Peter's wrists.

Then the angel said to him, "Put on your clothes and sandals." And Peter did so. "Wrap your cloak around you and follow me," the angel told him. Peter followed him out of the prison, but he had no idea that what the angel was doing was really happening; he thought he was seeing a vision. They passed the first and second guards and came to the iron gate leading to the city. It opened for them by itself, and they went through it. When they had walked the length of one street, suddenly the angel left him.

Then Peter came to himself and said, "Now I know without a doubt that the Lord sent his angel and rescued me from Herod's clutches and from everything the Jewish people were anticipating."

When this had dawned on him, he went to the house of Mary the mother of John, also called Mark, where many people had gathered and were praying. Peter knocked at the outer entrance, and a servant girl named Rhoda came to answer the door. When she recognized Peter's voice, she was so overjoyed she ran back without opening it and exclaimed, "Peter is at the door!"

"You're out of your mind," they told her. When she kept insisting that it was so, they said, "It must be his angel."

But Peter kept on knocking, and when they opened the door and saw him, they were astonished. Peter motioned with his hand for them to be quiet and described how the Lord had brought him out of prison. "Tell James and the brothers about this," he said, and then he left for another place.

In the morning, there was no small commotion among the soldiers as to what had become of Peter. After Herod had a thorough search made for him and did not find him, he cross-examined the guards and ordered that they be executed.

Prayer Partners Are Essential

Verse 5 is an important verse in this passage: "So Peter was kept in prison, *but the church was earnestly praying to God for him*" (emphasis added). So too is verse 12: "When this had dawned on him [when Peter realized that he had been set free], "he went to the house of Mary the mother of John, also called Mark, *where many people had gathered and were praying*" (emphasis added).

Prayer partners are essential. God has created us for relationship with Him and with other believers. The early church understood the reality that we need strong relationships with other believers. When Peter was in prison and was about to be put on trial and very likely was going to be killed for being obedient to God, it was at this critical point in his life that God's children got together and began to pray.

Do you have some prayer partners? Do you have people with whom you can trust the innermost secrets of your heart? Do you have people who will pray with you and who will be with you through thick and thin? Another important question: is there anyone who can count on you as their prayer partner? Are you the kind of Christian others can turn to and share their heart? If someone wants to share something with you that they don't want anyone else to know, can they trust you? Prayer partners work both ways. I am so thankful that I have some people I can go to and share my heart with, and I am thankful that those people know they can come to me and share their heart as well.

Why do we need prayer partners?

1. *We are not strong enough alone.* As much as we want to think we are, we are not strong enough. God wants us to realize this because He wants us to depend on Him and on others.
2. *We are not wise enough.* Although as Christians we have God living in us through the Holy Spirit, we must also realize that often God speaks to us through other believers. God wants us to spend time connecting with other believers as a way of hearing from Him.
3. *We are not consistent enough.* The truth is that we tend to be inconsistent. Prayer partners help us stay consistent and on target with what God is saying and doing.

Prayer Partners Encourage Us

Acts 12:5 is such an encouraging verse: "So Peter was kept in prison, but the church was earnestly praying to God for him." The word *earnestly* gives us an indication that the Christians weren't just praying a simple little prayer on Peter's behalf. They were earnestly praying for him. *Earnestly* carries with it the idea of praying with a deep committed desire.

As the Christians were praying earnestly, they were encouraging one another. I can imagine that as one person was praying for Peter and was becoming upset and brokenhearted over Peter's being in prison, another Christian was there with his hand on that believer's shoulder, patting him on the back, encouraging him as he prayed. I've been in prayer circles where the person voicing the prayer had everyone else in that prayer circle lifting them up in prayer. We need others lifting us up. When all we do is go to our prayer closet alone (and everyone should go to their prayer closet to pray) and never participate in praying with partners, we miss interacting with others and receiving the encouragement we need.

Exodus 17 tells the story of a battle. Joshua was leading the fight, and Moses was to keep his arms held up with his staff in the air. As long as Moses kept his staff in the air, Israel was experiencing victory: "So Joshua fought the Amalekites as Moses had ordered, and Moses, Aaron and Hur went to the top of the hill. As long as Moses held up his hands, the Israelites were winning, but whenever he lowered his hands, the Amalekites were winning. When Moses' hands grew tired, they took a stone and put it under him and he sat on it. Aaron and Hur held his hands up—one on one side, one on the other—so that his hands remained steady till sunset. So Joshua overcame the Amalekite army with the sword" (vv. 10–13).

Why did Joshua and the Israelites win the battle? God blessed them with victory because when Moses' arms got heavy and weak, Aaron stood on one side of Moses and Hur stood on the other side, and they held up his arms, encouraging him as Joshua led the battle on the field. That is an incredible picture of how prayer partners can encourage each other. Sometimes we need to hold up someone else's arms. Sometimes we need to slip a seat beneath the one needing help. Sometimes all the other person needs is a little encouragement.

We need prayer partners to encourage us:

1. *Because sometimes we get depressed.* Almost everyone gets depressed. Every person I've ever known would tell me that at one point or more in their lives, they knew they were experiencing some depression. It might not have been clinical depression, but they were depressed about something. That happens to us simply because we are human beings. We need people with us to encourage us.

2. *Because sometimes we feel hopeless.* Have you ever gone through a situation and you felt as if there was no way out, and you felt hopeless? As you look back at the situation five years later, you think, wow, it really wasn't that bad, but at the time, it felt as if it were the end of the world! I love the movie *It's a Wonderful Life*; I watch it every year. I wish there were a way you could go back to show those who have committed suicide what could have been. Many people who have attempted suicide have gone on to live wonderful and fulfilled lives, and they look back years later and say, thank you, God; thank you for not letting me be successful at killing myself. We just don't know. There are times when things seem hopeless, and we need to be there

with each other, to encourage each other, to strengthen each other, and to provide a sense of hope to one another.

3. *Because sometimes we need to be lifted up, like Moses was.* Prayer partners are there to lift us up. I believe that is what the early church was doing. They were lifting each other up, even as they were lifting Peter up in prayer. We need to be lifted up by others, and others need us to lift them up.

Prayer Partners Keep Us Focused

The church was praying diligently. As a matter of fact, they were praying so diligently that when the knock came on the door, only one of them went to answer it. Rhoda went to the door and heard Peter's voice, and she was so excited that instead of unlocking the door (they had the door bolted shut because they were afraid that they might be arrested), she went back and told everybody else that Peter was at the door. And they told her she was nuts! They thought she had gone crazy. They even said it must be his angel. There was a Jewish superstition that every individual had his own guardian angel (and that may or may not be the case, as God's Word appears to allude to that in several places), and that sometimes that guardian angel could even take on the appearance of the person they were guarding. So they thought, maybe that is Peter's angel. Some of those gathered might have thought Peter had already been killed and it was just his spirit coming back. They didn't know what was going on, but they thought for sure it couldn't be Peter; after all, he was in prison. Have you ever prayed and asked God for something, and when God gave it to you, you were so surprised that you almost missed it? That's what happened here. They were so focused on praying that they forgot that God really could answer their prayers.

Prayer partners help us remember what we might have forgotten to pray about. Have you ever told someone you would pray for them and then forgot to do it? Prayer partners can remind us to pray.

There are times when we forget to look to God in prayer. Sometimes our prayers become nothing more than simply a complaint session. Sometimes we forget to look to God, and prayer partners help keep us focused on God more than on the problem.

As we pray, we should remove as many distractions as we possibly can. We should turn off our telephones, our televisions, and our radios. We should go to a place where we will not be bothered. And yet, sometimes we will still face distractions. The devil will use anything he can to distract us from praying effectively. Prayer partners can help us stay focused.

Prayer Partners Hold Us Accountable

There are times when we allow the busyness of our lives to overwhelm us and we fail to pray like we should. We need someone to hold us accountable. In Acts 12 the church had gathered together and were holding each other accountable. They were committed to asking God for a miracle on Peter's behalf. As they prayed together, they were holding one another accountable for what God had called them to do, which was to pray.

In 3 John 2–4, we read, "Dear friend, I pray that you may enjoy good health and that all may go well with you, even as your soul is getting along well. It gave me great joy to have some brothers come and tell about your faithfulness to the truth and how you continue to walk in the truth. I have no greater joy than to hear that my children are walking in the truth."

Prayer partners who hold us accountable help us walk in the truth. Do you have a prayer partner who is willing to ask you what you have been look-ing at on the computer? Do you have a prayer partner who is willing to ask you what kind of movies and television shows you have been watching? Do you have a prayer partner who is willing to ask you how faithful you have been — not just physically but even in your mind and heart — to your spouse and to your children? We need prayer partners who will hold us accountable both for the way we live and for how we should pray. For most of us, when times get tough, we are prone to say "forget it." Sometimes we cannot handle the pressure anymore. We need a prayer partner to help us keep going.

Prayer Partners Rejoice with Us

At the end of the day, when God does His great work, prayer partners give us someone to rejoice with. When the church finally realized that Peter was at the door and alive, they were able to rejoice with him and with each other in the fact that God had worked a miracle.

How much of a miracle was it? It was such a miracle that Peter, chained by guards with sentries at the gate, was able to have his chains removed, able to walk out right by the guards, and able to go through the iron gate. Peter just walked up and the iron gate opened for him. How miraculous was it? It was so miraculous that the only explanation those brothers and sisters in Christ had, the only possible explanation, was that Almighty God had worked a miracle, and together they rejoiced.

Are you going through anything in your life right now that could have a good outcome only if Almighty God works a miracle? You had better have some partners praying with you about that situation. When it is all said and done and God works that miracle, you will have someone to celebrate with, even if it's only a handful of people, rejoicing with them in what God has done.

The Importance of Writing Our Prayers with Our Partners

Just as essential as having prayer partners is writing out some of our prayers with our partners. An amazing thing occurs when we write something down. We begin to think about the situation in a deeper and more meaningful way. We are forced to look at what we are saying or requesting.

Just as prayer partners encourage us, so too does the process of writing out our prayers. We will be encouraged by seeing the written request or praise.

Writing out our prayers with our partners will also assist us in staying focused on the matter at hand. Prayer is communion with God, and writing out what is on our hearts helps us stay on target with what God has led us to do with our prayer partners.

One last benefit of writing out our prayers with our partners is that it gives us a record we can go back to. It is an incredible blessing to read over a prayer journal with a partner we have prayed with and rejoice together in God's answers to prayer. Sometimes the rejoicing is over the fact that although God did not answer the prayer in the manner we had desired, we now have the benefit of hindsight to reflect and see that His answer was indeed far better than the answer we had hoped for. Having the written record with your prayer partner makes this type of celebration possible.

Conclusion

It is fun being a Christian. It is great fun watching God work miracles. It is exciting to see God do the seemingly impossible. Experience the power of praying with partners. Find some good Christian friends whom you can trust and with whom you will pray regularly. This will give your prayer life a whole new dimension. It will never again be the same.

Are you willing to let God do something great in your life today? Are you willing to let God work miracles in and through your life? Develop some prayer partners with whom you will team up, and begin praying together today.

Allow me to share one word of caution. Praying together is an incredibly intense and emotional experience. We know that the devil desires to destroy us any way he can. One of the key temptations he uses is sexual temptation. My advice is not to have someone of the opposite sex, other than your spouse, be your prayer partner. There are too many possible negatives that can arise, and there are plenty of opportunities to pray with the opposite sex in small-group and corporate settings that do not present the same temptation.

In the space on the following page, list the people God places on your heart to contact concerning being your prayer partners:

Using Written Prayers in a Small Group

An important part of the Christian life is not only praying alone and with partners but also praying with fellow believers in a small-group setting. Prayer partners provide a sense of encouragement, accountability, focus, and other positive attributes. As great as these are, these positives can be magnified to a much greater degree in a small group. This small group could be your family, a Bible study group, a Sunday school class, a men's or ladies' prayer group, a youth group, or some other small group whose purpose is to pray.

In Acts 12, small-group prayer is modeled for us. Unlike many prayer meetings that occur today, this gathering was more about praying than meeting. Far too much time is spent in many churches and small-group prayer meetings today simply talking about praying. But these believers got together and they prayed. The key for our small groups is to make sure prayer is the purpose. Don't get me wrong, there can be other purposes for small groups, such as studying the Bible, discussing important issues, and even planning and implementing fun activities. But if we are going to have a small group whose purpose is to pray, we need to make sure we pray.

Sometimes a small group can easily be led off track by one person who has an agenda he feels compelled to share with everyone else. It is because of situations like this that it's important to have a written prayer agenda to begin the meeting with. This will help ensure that the meeting focuses on praying and not just meeting. Having an agenda is not intended to prevent the Holy Spirit from leading the group to pray in any direction He chooses; it is simply a tool to help us remember why we gathered in the first place.

Another challenge we often face is spending so much time talking about the need to pray that we don't really spend any time praying. As important as it is to make sure everyone knows what we need to pray about, it is of the utmost importance that we actually pray. I have been in prayer meetings where ten times as much time was spent discussing the need to pray as was spent praying. This is not what the early church appeared to do.

One possible solution to the problem of having prayer discussions and requests take more time than they should involves the use of email. Most people today have some connection to email either at their home, office, local library, or a friend's house. If the small-group prayer meeting is scheduled to begin at 7:00 p.m., have each person who is aware of a prayer request or praise email that to one person by 4:00 p.m. This will allow that person time to gather the requests and praises and print them out for all of the group members. Although there will be some items added later, collecting most beforehand greatly reduces the amount of time required to discuss people's requests and provides more time for praying about those requests.

In addition to emailing requests and praises, some groups also have a computer and printer set up at the site of the prayer gathering. This allows any additional requests and praises to be added to the list at the beginning of the gathering so each participant will know exactly what they are praying for.

As we begin to pray in our small groups, it is a great help to also have some of our prayers written out. The same positives that exist for writing out prayers with our prayer partners exist for writing them out with our small group — they are simply magnified. Below you will find several suggestions for implementing written prayers with a small group.

- *Written prayers as a team.* This could be a meaningful and even fun activity for a Sunday school class or other small group to do. Each person in the small group writes a portion of the prayer. One person begins, and then each participant, either in a predetermined or an extemporaneous order, adds to the prayer as God leads. In this form of praying, the small group allows God to speak to and through each participant concerning a certain topic.

- *Written prayers for one another in a small group.* One way to do this is to have everyone in the group write his or her name and a prayer need or praise on a slip of paper. Then each person draws a slip of paper and writes a letter to God as a prayer on behalf of the person whose slip of paper they drew. Our women's ministry group did this once in a really unique way at a recent women's event. They placed small, gift-wrapped boxes on each table. The ladies each took a box and wrote her name on the bottom. Then they exchanged boxes. The ladies were instructed to write a prayer of encouragement for the person whose name they received. Then they hung the boxes on a Christmas tree, where every time they saw them, they were reminded to pray. The ladies also were encouraged to write their prayers to God and send them to the person they were praying for. Although the prayer was to God and not the person, the ladies received such a blessing from knowing that someone else cared for them and had taken the time to express this prayer to God on their behalf.

- *Written prayers for each member of your family.* Why not keep a separate journal for each member of your family, filled with letters to God on their behalf? What a treasure to be able to share that journal with them one day!

- *Another version of the written prayers for your family.* Have a time each night or maybe once a week when each member of the family writes a letter to God for another member of the family. Rotate who writes the prayer for whom so everyone has the opportunity to pray for each other and everyone is prayed for by everyone else regularly. Instead of waiting until a later time to share the journal with them, give the letters to each person each time they are written. Even if they have to have help writing out their prayers, young children will enjoy participating, and this is a great way to model prayer for your family.

- *Written prayers penned by one person and shared by a small group.* In this method of praying, one person writes the prayer, and each member of the group participates in voicing the prayer. This is similar to a method mentioned previously, but it involves only one person actually doing the writing. Some people are self-conscious about their penmanship, and this method removes that concern while allowing each person in the small group the opportunity of sharing their heart in the prayer time.

Some topics for letters to God by your small group:

- *Praise.* Spend time in your small group writing letters of praise to God. Give Him glory and honor for how wonderful and awesome He is. Be creative in writing these letters of praise, and use the Bible as your primary source for attributes of praise to share with God.
- *Thanksgiving.* Write letters of thanks to God. These letters may be in reference to your small group, or they may be unique to each participant or even in reference to a larger group of people. The key here is to spend time thanking God. We have so much to be thankful for. We often talk about how thankful we should be, and this method helps us to practice what we say we should do.
- *Confession.* Use some of your small-group prayer time confessing sin to God and writing these confessions down. The only concern here is that each person in the small group must understand the importance of confidentiality. There are certain things you need not share except with a very small group of trusted friends and prayer partners, but there are enough sins we all share in common that we can spend significant time confessing and repenting of these in our small-group gatherings.
- *Petition.* As you pray in your small group, include prayers of petition. Be transparent enough to pray for your own needs. One of our biggest problems is that we do not allow anyone to see who we are and what we are struggling with, and because of that, no one knows how to pray for us. When we are humble enough to pray for ourselves in our small-group gathering and actually write down our needs on paper, it sends the message that we truly understand how much we depend on God. Again, there will be certain things that we will need to pray for only with a very small group of trusted friends and prayer partners, but prayers of petition are a great need for us.
- *Intercession.* One of the most wonderful gifts we have been given is the gift of praying for another person. Make sure your small-group prayer time includes the practice of interceding for one another. Writing out your heartfelt prayers for others in your small group will bless you as well as them. Each person needs prayer, and when others see that your group is serious about praying for one another, they will be encouraged to pray more as well. Occasionally give the written prayer to the person for whom you prayed as a way of reminding them that they are loved and cared for.

Using Written Prayers in a Congregation

The two subjects sure to tickle the typical evangelical's guilt-bone are evangelism and prayer. We love to speak of the power of prayer and affirm its importance for the church, but seldom do our professed values translate into attendance of and engagement with the prayer gatherings of the local body. Most pastors know that the most lightly attended services often are those that feature prayer as the main ingredient. My primary experience has been with what some call free prayer as opposed to written prayer. One of the key arguments in favor of free prayer over written prayer is that when a written prayer is read, it does not allow the Holy Spirit to move as freely as He should. If this argument is taken to its logical conclusion, however, one would have to be against singing written songs or even considering beforehand what one would pray about. A pastor would have to be opposed to preparing anything ahead of time to preach. The truth is that the same Holy Spirit who leads the songwriter to pen the words to a song or who leads a pastor to develop and write a powerful message is able to lead a believer to write a prayer before it is time for it to be offered in a public setting.

Written prayer can be a valuable and powerful part of a corporate worship experience. Throughout history Christians have expressed prayer both verbally and in written form. At times the written prayers are read individually, and at times they are read corporately during a public worship service. These prayers are sometimes read silently, and sometimes they are read aloud. Sharing written prayer corporately can help build unity and focus for a church family.

Some examples of using written prayer corporately:

- Leading members in writing their own prayer letters to God.
- Members reading aloud previously written prayers.
- A pastor or another leader reading aloud prayers written specifically for the church family.
- Singing written prayers as congregational songs.
- Including written prayers as part of a concert of prayer corporate worship experience.

Remember to be sensitive to the different prayer traditions that people come from. As it's appropriate, use some of the following forms:

1. A leader praying on behalf of the whole group.
2. Silent prayer to confess personal sin or offer personal requests.

3. Community prayer (be sure instructions are clear and that everyone understands the style and procedure):
   a. *Cambridge style.* Several people lead, ending each prayer with "In Jesus' name," and then everyone joins in with "amen."
   b. *Conversational style.* Usually better for small groups. Several people lead in short informal prayers, moving from one topic to another.
   c. *Scripture prayers.* Many people lead out in short prayers of praise, confession, and so on.
   d. *Liturgical prayers.* Using the Lord's Prayer or written prayers to pray in unison.
   e. *Small-group prayer.* Dividing the people into small groups to pray. This can encourage greater participation, but be sensitive to non-Christians and visitors. Don't put them in a situation where they are forced to pray.

Cautions to consider:

- Be careful to take writing the prayer seriously, never frivolously.
- Write the prayer only to God, not as a message to others who will hear or read it.
- Never equate your written prayer with the Word of God.
- Do not rush the writing of your prayer.
- Always listen to what God is saying to you about yourself as you write your prayer.

One of the simplest ways to incorporate written prayer into a corporate worship service is to provide space, either in the bulletin or program for the service or by having blank paper available, for people (at a designated time in the service) to be led step by step to write a letter to God. For some, the concept will be foreign. Compare the different parts of a friendly letter (the greeting, the body, the closing) to different parts of a letter to God. As you discuss each part, give several examples and instruct the congregation to write their own greeting, body, and closing. Once they see how easy it is to do, and how meaningful it is, they will want to continue the practice. You could even set up a mailbox temporarily as a reminder to write letters to God. This is such a great way to spark the prayer life of your congregation!

The following is an outline of a concert of prayer I have led in several worship services. Consider using it, or something similar, for a corporate worship experience.

Sample Concert of Prayer

Prelude

Play worship music softly in the background.
"Please enter in an attitude of prayer and spiritual preparation."

Congregational Praise in Preparation for Prayer

"Shine, Jesus, Shine," by Graham Kendrick
"If My People's Hearts Are Humbled," by Claire Cloninger
"Heal Our Land," by Tom Brooks
"Revive Us, O Lord," by Carman

Prayer and Scriptural Preparation

If my people, who are called by my name, will humble themselves and pray and seek my face and turn from their wicked ways, then will I hear from heaven and will forgive their sin and will heal their land.

— 2 Chronicles 7:14

Sow for yourselves righteousness,
    reap the fruit of unfailing love,
and break up your unplowed ground;
    for it is time to seek the LORD,
until he comes
    and showers righteousness on you.
— Hosea 10:12

"Even now," declares the LORD,
    "return to me with all your heart,
with fasting and weeping and mourning."

Rend your heart
    and not your garments.
Return to the LORD your God,
    for he is gracious and compassionate,
slow to anger and abounding in love,
    and he relents from sending calamity.
— Joel 2:12 – 13

Prayer of Praise and Thanksgiving

Read chorally, then allow individuals time to write their own prayers in the space provided. Play worship music softly in the background.

Our dear loving and awesome God,
We praise You for who You are. You are absolutely incredible; there is no one and nothing like You. You are all-powerful, all-knowing, and always present. Thank you for Your gift of salvation and for every other gift You have provided, including our families, church, and nation. We acknowledge our complete dependence on You.
In Jesus' name, amen

Dear God,

In Jesus' name, amen

Congregational Praise Time

"Change My Heart, O God," by Eddie Espinosa

"Seekers of Your Heart," by Beverly Darnall, Dick Tunney, and Melodie Tunney

"O Lord, You're Beautiful," by Keith Green

"As the Deer," by Martin Nystrom

"Sanctuary," by John W. Thompson and Randy Scruggs

Scriptural Preparation

If I had cherished sin in my heart,
    the Lord would not have listened.
                                        —Psalm 66:18

Surely the arm of the LORD is not too short to save,
    nor his ear too dull to hear.
But your iniquities have separated
    you from your God;
your sins have hidden his face from you,
    so that he will not hear.
                                        —Isaiah 59:1–2

Therefore confess your sins to each other and pray for each other so that you may be healed. The prayer of a righteous man is powerful and effective.
                                        —James 5:16

Prayers of Confession and Repentance

Read chorally, then allow individuals to write their own prayers in the space provided. Encourage individuals to be specific as they confess their sins to God. Play worship music softly in the background.

Dear Heavenly Father,
    We come before You to confess our sins. We have sinned against You in our hearts and actions. We begin the process of repentance as we turn our hearts toward You.
    In Jesus' name, amen

Dear God,

In Jesus' name, amen

Worship and Praise for God's Cleansing

If we confess our sins, he is faithful and just and will forgive us our sins and purify us from all unrighteousness.

—1 John 1:9

Prayers of Thanksgiving for God's Cleansing

Read chorally, then allow individuals to write their own prayers in the space provided. Play worship music softly in the background.

Dear God,

It is an incredible blessing to know that You provide forgiveness and cleansing for us. As dirty as we are because of our sin, You make us as clean as pure white snow. Oh God, please help us remember how filthy we are without You and how spotless we are through Your Son.

In Jesus' name, amen

Dear God,

In Jesus' name, amen

Scriptural Preparation for a Time of Intercession and Petition

Therefore I will give him a portion among the great,
  and he will divide the spoils with the strong,
because he poured out his life unto death,
  and was numbered with the transgressors.
For he bore the sin of many,
  and made intercession for the transgressors.
  —Isaiah 53:12

I urge, then, first of all, that requests, prayers, intercession and thanksgiving be made for everyone.
  —1 Timothy 2:1

In the same way, the Spirit helps us in our weakness. We do not know what we ought to pray for, but the Spirit himself intercedes for us with groans that words cannot express. And he who searches our hearts knows the mind of the Spirit, because the Spirit intercedes for the saints in accordance with God's will.
  —Romans 8:26–27

Therefore he is able to save completely those who come to God through him, because he always lives to intercede for them.
  —Hebrews 7:25

Do not be anxious about anything, but in everything, by prayer and petition, with thanksgiving, present your requests to God.
  —Philippians 4:6

Prayers of Intercession and Petition for Personal, Family, Church, and National Revival

Read chorally, then allow individuals to write their own prayers in the space provided. For this period of written prayer, provide several spaces for different prayers. Play worship music softly in the background.

Dear Almighty God,

We come before You to intercede on behalf of those we know and love, as well as for those who act as enemies toward us. Please protect our church family and our own families. Please provide courage, wisdom, and strength for every day. We also pray for ourselves that we will faithfully obey You at all times.

In Jesus' name, amen

Dear God,

In Jesus' name, amen

The Hymn of Response

"I Surrender All," by Judson W. Van DeVenter and Winfield S. Weeden

Notes

1. Bingham Hunter, *The God Who Hears* (Downers Grove, Ill.: InterVarsity, 1986), 39.
2. Centers for Disease Control and Prevention, "Youth Risk Behavior Surveillance — United States, 2007," *Surveillance Summaries*, vol. 58, no. SS–4 (June 6, 2008), table 61, *http://www.cdc.gov/HealthyYouth/yrbs/pdf/yrbss07_mmwr.pdf* (September 2, 2008).
3. Centers for Disease Control and Prevention, "HPV Vaccine Information for Young Women," *Sexually Transmitted Diseases* (June 26, 2008), *http://www.cdc.gov/std/hpv/STDFact-HPV-vaccine-young-women.htm#hpvvac1*.
4. Office of Juvenile Justice and Delinquency Prevention, *Drinking in America: Myths, Realities, and Prevention Policy* (Washington, D.C.: U.S. Department of Justice, Office of Justice Programs, Office of Juvenile Justice and Delinquency Prevention, 2005), *http://www.udetc.org/documents/Drinking_in_America.pdf*.
5. Substance Abuse and Mental Health Services Administration, *Drug Abuse Warning Network, 2005: National Estimates of Drug-Related Emergency Department Visits*, DAWN series D–29, DHHS no. (SMA) 07–4256; 2007 (Rockville, Md.: Substance Abuse and Mental Health Services Administration, Office of Applied Studies), *http://www.ci.findlay.oh.us/uploads/File/Health/Health%20Assessment/Assessment%202003/L-Hancock%20Youth%20Alcohol.pdf*.
6. "Violence: Fast Facts," *Teen Health and the Media* (Seattle, Wash.: Univ. of Washington), *http://depts.washington.edu/thmedia/view.cgi?section=violence&page=fastfacts*.
7. *Third International Mathematics and Science Study: Highlights*, table 1, "Mathematics and Science Literacy" (Chestnut Hill, Mass.: Boston College, February 1998), *http://timss.bc.edu/timss1995i/TIMSSPDF/C_Hilite.pdf* (April 27, 2004).
8. College Parents of America, "A Conversation with James A. Boyle" (Oct. 20, 2009), *http://www.collegeparents.org/cpa/about-boyle_conversation.html*.
9. Learn more about Moms in Touch at *http://momsintouch.org*.

10. Richard Land, "Your Prayers Can Change Our Country" (Jan. 12, 2009), The Ethics and Religious Liberty Commission, *http://erlc.com/article/your-prayers-can-change-our-country/*.

11. C. Hoyt Watson, *The Amazing Story of Sergeant Jacob DeShazer* (Winona Lake, Ind.: Light and Life Press, 1950), 122.

André K. Dugger resides in the Nashville, Tennessee, area with his wife, Sarah, and their six children. He has served as the pastor of Grace Baptist Church of Nashville since 1997. André has published articles in several magazines and has authored several books, including the devotional gift book *Dear God*. He is a frequent speaker at conferences and seminars and enjoys sharing his passionate love for God. Discover more about André and keep up with him on the web at *www.andredugger.com*. To request André for a speaking engagement, contact him via email: akdugger@aol.com.

READ. WRITE. REPEAT.

More products inspired by the
major motion picture letters to God

LETTERS TO GOD - THE NOVEL (ISBN: 9780310327653)
Now read the book behind the movie for a closer look at Tyler's story.

PRAYER: YOUR OWN LETTER TO GOD (ISBN: 9780310327639)
Strengthen your relationship with God. One prayer at a time.

LETTERS TO GOD - BIBLE (ISBN: 9780310949435)
This special Bible used in the movie features handwritten notes
and underlined verses to help you better understand Scripture.

LETTERS TO GOD - PICTURE BOOK (ISBN: 9780310720133)
Spark a child's imagination with this picture book based on the movie.

LETTERS TO GOD - JOURNAL (ISBN: 9780310720027)
Take your prayer to a new level by writing your own letters to God.

HOPE IS CONTAGIOUS (ISBN: 9780310327684)
Shows how to experience and spread hope in the face of every obstacle.

DEAR GOD (ISBN: 9780310327738)
Read Tyler's letters and get inspired to dig deeper into your faith.

For more information or to purchase these products
visit www.Zondervan.com or your local bookseller.

Share Your Thoughts

With the Author: Your comments will be forwarded to the author when you send them to *zauthor@zondervan.com*.

With Zondervan: Submit your review of this book by writing to *zreview@zondervan.com*.

Free Online Resources at
www.zondervan.com

Zondervan AuthorTracker: Be notified whenever your favorite authors publish new books, go on tour, or post an update about what's happening in their lives at www.zondervan.com/authortracker.

Daily Bible Verses and Devotions: Enrich your life with daily Bible verses or devotions that help you start every morning focused on God. Visit www.zondervan.com/newsletters.

Free Email Publications: Sign up for newsletters on Christian living, academic resources, church ministry, fiction, children's resources, and more. Visit www.zondervan.com/newsletters.

Zondervan Bible Search: Find and compare Bible passages in a variety of translations at www.zondervanbiblesearch.com.

Other Benefits: Register yourself to receive online benefits like coupons and special offers, or to participate in research.

■ ZONDERVAN®

ZONDERVAN.com/
AUTHORTRACKER
follow your favorite authors